COVENANT • BIBLE • STUDIES

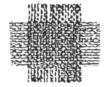

Daniel

Frank Ramirez

faithQuest® ♦ Brethren Press®

Covenant Bible Studies Series

Unless otherwise noted, scripture quotations are from the New Revised Standard Version of the Bible, copyrighted 1989 by the National Council of Churches
of Christ in the USA, Division of Education and Ministry.

Cover photo: D. Jeanene Tiner

02   01   00   99   98   5   4   3   2   1

Library of Congress Cataloging-in-Publication Data
Ramirez, Frank, 1954-
    Daniel / Frank Ramirez.
        p.   cm. --(Covenant Bible studies)
    ISBN 0-87178-012-7 (alk. paper)
        1. Bible. O.T. Daniel--Study and teaching.   I. Title.
        II. Series: Covenant Bible study series.
    BS1555.5.R36 1998
    224′.5′007--dc21   97-35842

Manufactured in the United States of America

Contents

Foreword

The Covenant Bible Studies Series was first developed for a denominational program in the Church of the Brethren and the Christian Church (Disciples of Christ). This program, called People of the Covenant, was founded on the concept of relational Bible study and has been adopted by several other denominations and small groups who want to study the Bible in a community rather than alone.

Relational Bible study is marked by certain characteristics, some of which differ from other types of Bible study. For one, it is intended for small groups of people who can meet face-to-face on a regular basis and share frankly with an intimate group.

It is important to remember that relational Bible study is anchored in covenantal history. God covenanted with people in Old Testament history, established a new covenant in Jesus Christ, and covenants with the church today.

Relational Bible study takes seriously a corporate faith. As each person contributes to study, prayer, and work, the group becomes the real body of Christ. Each one's contribution is needed and important. "For just as the body is one and has many members, and all the members of the body, though many, are one body, so it is with Christ. . . . Now you are the body of Christ and individually members of it" (1 Cor. 12:12,17).

Relational Bible study helps both individuals and the group to claim the promise of the Spirit and the working of the Spirit. As one person testified, "In our commitment to one another and in our sharing, something happened. . . . We were woven together in love by the Master Weaver. It is something that can happen only when two or three or seven are gathered in God's name, and we know the promise of God's presence in our lives."

The symbol of these covenant Bible study groups is the burlap cross. The interwoven threads, the uniqueness of each strand, the unrefined fabric, and the rough texture characterize covenant groups. The people in the groups are unique but interrelated; they are imperfect and unpolished, but loving and supportive.

The shape that these divergent threads create is the cross, the symbol for all Christians of the resurrection and presence with us of Christ our

Savior. Like the burlap cross, we are brought together, simple and ordinary, to be sent out again in all directions to be in the world.

For people who choose to use this study in a small group, the following guidelines will help create an atmosphere in which support will grow and faith will deepen.

1. As a small group of learners, we gather around God's word to discern its meaning for today.
2. The words, stories, and admonitions we find in scripture come alive for today, challenging and renewing us.
3. All people are learners and all are leaders.
4. Each person will contribute to the study, sharing the meaning found in the scripture and helping to bring meaning to others.
5. We recognize each other's vulnerability as we share out of our own experience, and in sharing we learn to trust others and to be trustworthy.

Additional suggestions for study and group-building are provided in the "Sharing and Prayer" section. They are intended for use in the hour preceding the Bible study to foster intimacy in the covenant group and relate personal sharing to the Bible study topic.

Welcome to this study. As you search the scriptures, may you also search yourself. May God's voice and guidance and the love and encouragement of brothers and sisters in Christ challenge you to live more fully the abundant life God promises.

Recommended Resources

Collins, John. *Daniel* (Hermaneia Commentary). Augsburg Fortress, 1994.

Goldingay, John. *Daniel* (Biblical Commentary Series). Word, 1989.

Hartman, Louis F. and Alexander A. Di Lella. *The Book of Daniel* (Anchor Bible Commentary). Doubleday, 1978.

Lederach, Paul. *Daniel* (Believers Church Bible Commentary Series). Herald Press, 1995.

New Interpreter's Bible, Vol. VII. "Introduction to Apocalyptic Literature, Daniel, The Twelve Prophets." Abingdon, 1996.

Preface

In 170 B.C., Antiochus, king of the Seleucid empire, attacked Egypt and overtook its cowardly and weak ruler, Ptolemy VI. The young and brave neighboring Roman republic didn't want Seleucid competition on the Mediterranean Sea, however, so it ordered Antiochus and his forces out of Egypt. Forced to comply, the humiliated Antiochus looked for someone on whom to take revenge.

The Judeans, who had been well treated by the Egyptians, were perhaps too jubilant about Antiochus's humiliation. They became the target of Seleucid revenge. In the year 167 B.C., Antiochus invaded Jerusalem. He desecrated the Jewish temple by sacrificing a pig to the god Zeus on the sacred altar, an act so horrible the Jews had to invent a new term to express it, Abomination of Desolation.

Unlike the Persian emperor who ruled Judea and tolerated its religion, Antiochus forbade all practice of Israelite religion. He attempted to stamp out Jewish practices, torturing and killing those who stayed faithful to God's ways. The tribulation became more than many could bear. Some fled to the hills. Many were killed. And some cooperated with their new masters and worshiped new gods.

Where there is suppression, there is often resistance. Using guerrilla tactics, a group of Jews called the Maccabees, followers of Judas Maccabeus, eventually drove the foreign oppressors from Judah and for the first time in centuries established a free and autonomous Jewish state. The Maccabees saw history as an armed conflict on behalf of God.

At the same time, another group of Jews, perhaps called the Wise Ones, felt that trust in God and nonviolent resistance would lead to victory. After all, God had acted on their behalf before, rescuing a nation of slaves from Egypt and leading them through the desert to the promised land. There was also God's judgment of Israel, exiling the people to Babylon, but he later redeemed them. If the Wise Ones waited on God, they knew they would be delivered from the hand of the new oppressor.

Which view is correct—that of the Maccabees, or the one belonging to the Wise Ones? To this day there is no general agreement. The freedom that came from the Maccabean revolt lasted less than a century, but it was real. The faith of the Wise Ones that God controls history has endured, even in this century—a century that has seen two world wars, genocide, and nuclear and chemical weapons. It has witnessed Gandhi's and King's nonviolent revolutions, the fall of the iron curtain and apartheid, and the development of international law. What are the limits of force? What is the potential of nonviolent resistance?

The Book of Daniel is set against the background of the Babylonian exile, but it was written during the time of the Maccabean revolt. Its message, however, is not the Maccabean message. Daniel's message is "Hold on! Help is on the way!" God is in control of history, and in God's time everything will be worked out. God's people will shine like the stars once the verdict of history is in.

For many people today—the immigrant, the conquered, and the oppressed—the Book of Daniel is as relevant as it ever was. How do people live as strangers in a strange land, forced to change their names and customs and religion? Can they hold on until God helps them, or will they rise up?

Most readers of this book will not be living under active persecution. Still, how we look at things colors our experience of the world. Is the glass half empty or half full? Should we be activists for God, or is God an activist for us? Perhaps the answer lies somewhere between in a place you will discover for yourselves.

Note:
Eight of these ten lessons on Daniel include readings from the Apocrypha, a group of scriptures not included in the Old or New Testaments, but sometimes included in a separate section of the Bible. These include First and Second Maccabees, Judith, Tobit, Bel and the Dragon, Susanna, the Letter of Jeremiah, Baruch, and First Esdras. At one time these books were the common heritage of all Christians. After the Reformation, however, they were separated from the books of the Bible we know today and placed between the Old and New Testaments, which is appropriate since most of them originated in the "intertestamental period," the time between the last of the prophets and the birth of Jesus.

The Apocrypha is not included in all versions of the Bible. Consider borrowing Bibles that include the Apocrypha from friends or the library, or you may want to order inexpensive paperback Bibles that include the Apocrypha from a group such as the American Bible Society.

—Frank Ramirez

1

Enduring Together
Daniel 1

When his people are taken into Babylonian captivity, Daniel finds himself a servant of the enemy king. He shows that it's possible to be faithful even in the most difficult circumstances.

Personal Preparation

1. Before you read Daniel 1, recall stories of Daniel from your memory. Then read Daniel 1. Remember that Daniel lost his homeland, his name, and his identity. What have you lost over the course of time?
2. Draw a timeline of a difficult period in either your personal, family, or church life. How long did this difficult period last in relationship to your life? How were you able to get through it? How did you move through it?
3. Draw a timeline of your life's golden age. How long did this period last? Is it still going on? Were you aware of the quality of this time of your life when you were living it?

Understanding

The first time I ever ran a marathon I was afraid because I didn't know what to expect. The next six times I was afraid because I knew precisely what to expect. All seven times I ran the 26.2-mile race I experienced chemical depression between miles 16 and 20. The pain wasn't the problem. It was the feeling that none of it mattered. After mile twenty the race became easy. Even when I was reduced to walking and once to limping, it didn't matter. I knew how far I was from the end, and I felt great.

What I learned about distance running is true about a lot of life. If you know when the ordeal will end, you can take it. But what happens when there is no finish line? A woman at my church attends daily to her mother, who's been dying for two years now. Many times her mother has seemed close to death, but then she rallies and resumes a life that requires constant care. The daughter is learning to pace herself.

Then there's the mom who's been raising a daughter who has severe physical disabilities. She knows she will be caring for this child the rest of her life. And I often think of the man who cared for his wife with Alzheimers. He wasn't getting younger, and the care took a physical toll on him. Endurance is everything when you don't know when your trials will end.

In South Africa who among those living under apartheid could have predicted it would ever end? But endurance paid off. Their nation has chosen truth commissions over retribution.

Lord, How Long?

Life's real endurance races are run by those who suffer under adverse conditions with no end in sight. They need support and encouragement. They need to know God is on their side when they really feel like God has abandoned them altogether.

This is the case for Daniel's people, the Israelites living in exile in the sixth century before Christ. The Book of Daniel opens with the shattering loss of the land and the temple. A way of life for God's people seems to be coming to a close. The ancients believed that while armies fought on the earth, the gods fought in heaven. A defeat for one was a defeat for the other; so, by the logic of the day, Nebuchadnezzar's defeat of God's people means a defeat for the God of Israel as well.

The first chapter of Daniel sends a more hopeful message, however. It sets the scene and lets us know that no matter how bad things look, Daniel will survive the Babylonian exile. Relax. We learn how the sacred vessels got to Babylon. We see that allegiance is owed to God first and rulers second. And we learn that appearances are deceiving.

Daniel 1 even asserts it was God's will that the exile took place. One interpretation suggests that God's people were torn from their promised land because they had been unfaithful for centuries. The destruction of the temple, therefore, was a catastrophe for the people, but not for God.

Psalm 137, written about the anguish God's people felt when they were led away to Babylon, asks the question, "How can we sing the Lord's song in a foreign land?" This was a people who were grieving, and rightfully so, over the loss of everything they knew. It seemed impossible to them that they could go on. But they did.

As a whole society, we North Americans have never lost everything—our culture, our language, or our possessions. Even if our houses are destroyed by hurricane or flood or earthquake, even if a great portion of a community is reduced to matchsticks, the basic social structure of our culture remains, and with it some measure of hope.

But whole cultures and religious groups in other parts of the world have experienced the unutterable wrenching that occurs when everything is destroyed and people must flee. Some of these refugees have found a place in North America, and perhaps even in your congregation.

One of the most devastating losses for a group is the loss of a common language. Storyteller Garrison Keillor, writing of the Norwegian immigrants who settled in Minnesota, says that no one is ever as intelligent as when they are speaking in their native tongue. Invaders have known this for a long time. They can more easily conquer a culture if their captives are forbidden to use their own language. Without their own language, the customs and the identity of the conquered people soon fade and they become more compliant to the rules of society and the expressions of the invaders' language.

Looking back in U.S. history, we know that this is true. The United States government acculturated American Indians by separating children from their families and communities and forbidding them to speak their native languages. West Africans were wrenched from their homelands for slave trade in America, where they had to give up their own cultures and take on white culture, religion, and language. Some slave owners even took away names. Think about the names in your family and what they mean, and then imagine what life would be like without those names.

Even European cultures in the U.S. have experienced cultural pressure. Cincinnati was largely a German-speaking city until the outbreak of World War I in 1914 when cultural pressure led many German Americans to drop their mother tongue for English. And hispanic culture in the U.S., with its Mesoamerican twist, struggles mightily to resist the pressure to drop Spanish as a native language.

This gutting of native culture is precisely the experience of Daniel and his three companions. The Babylonians gave each of them new names and forced them to learn a new language in the king's court. Daniel (whose name means "God has judged") became Belteshazzar ("Bel guard his life"). Hananiah ("Yahweh has been gracious") was renamed Shadrach ("I am fearful of God"). Mishael ("Who is what God is?")

became Meshach ("I am of little account"). Azariah ("Yahweh has helped") was renamed Abednego ("Servant of the shining one," a reference to the god Nabu). In the ancient world, names reflected the essence of the person, and to rename someone was to cast away their old identity.

The Book of Daniel seems to say, in answer to Psalm 137, you can sing the Lord's song in a foreign land because God is not tied to one land or one temple. God is with you even in exile. At the end of the musical *Fiddler on the Roof*, when all the Jews are expelled from their Russian village, one character asks if this would be a good time for Messiah to come. The rabbi responds, saying they will all just have to continue to wait for Messiah in another place. Daniel and his companions continued to count on God's promises in another place as well.

But how do we live in occupied territory? How far can we go in serving secular rulers? In this story Daniel and the three young men dutifully serve masters in their new country, but they also recognize there are certain boundaries that cannot be crossed—in this case, they hold steadfastly to dietary laws whatever the consequences.

Daniel and his three companions accept their new names but they keep their old values, which include eating kosher foods. For example, it was a great honor to be asked to share the king's food, and the servant of the king is worried when the four Hebrews refuse. The rejection of hospitality, especially the king's, was considered a great insult.

One can assume the king's diet was probably loaded with fat and gunk. In ancient times many rich people suffered from gout because they regularly ate the sorts of food most people would eat only on feast days. Without question, the diet of Daniel and his companions had to be healthier than what would have been prepared in a king's kitchen.

God's lifestyle is designed to promote wholeness, shalom. Sticking to this lifestyle is a matter of faith for Daniel. It is like endurance. If we hold on to a godly lifestyle, it will pay off. God will win out eventually, even if it seems unlikely at the moment. Daniel is even willing to risk the consequences of insulting the king because he is confident not that God will save him, but that God will use him to eventually win out. Indeed, the lifestyle of the four companions is proven superior, and they are allowed to continue to serve the foreign king while remaining faithful to their religion.

At the end of the chapter, we read: "And Daniel continued there until the first year of King Cyrus." Despite their repressive power, tyrannies have limited life-spans. In some cases they do not even last the life of an individual. The mighty Soviet empire did not bury us, as one of its leaders promised. It ruled less than a human life-span. Hitler's Thousand

Year Reich fell more than nine hundred and ninety years short of its goal. And think of the dictators who have come and gone in our lifetime—Idi Amin, the Shah of Iran, Mao—not to mention some dictatorial policies of people considered to be democratic leaders. We will see that change is inevitable now as well as in Daniel's time.

Apocalyptic Now

The Book of Daniel is often misunderstood. Simply put, it was written for people of faith who were enduring times of trouble. And Daniel's message—Hold on!—is as clear for our times as his. But far from comforting the average Christian, Daniel is often treated as a strange and bizarre book with no connection to everyday life. Some insist the Book of Daniel is a road map of the future, a timeline for tribulation. Those who share this view believe they see this truth more clearly than others. Perhaps they believe God has revealed it to them or that they have special power to understand what others do not. They view themselves as part of a spiritual elite, members of a club with special insight.

In fact, no part of scripture is reserved for "special" people. The message of the Bible is for everyone. Elitist attitudes about scripture are sometimes the result of a misunderstanding about the nature of books of the Bible. If we take the books of the Bible at face value alone, several will no doubt seem very strange. On face value, Matthew and Malachi, Jude and Judges ought to be the same. But the books of the Bible are of different types, and knowing the type can tell us a lot about how to interpret them.

I chair a writers' group that meets twice a month. Members of our group read manuscripts aloud and critique them. One of the first things we ask the author is to what genre, or type, does this manuscript belong. That's because the rules are different for mystery, romance, science fiction, or biography. It is pointless to denounce a romance because it doesn't obey the rules of a mystery.

In coming to understand a book of the Bible, it helps if we know its genre. In the Old Testament, for instance, we are familiar with books of law, such as Leviticus; or the prophets, such as Jeremiah or Isaiah. Psalms and Song of Songs are poetry. Samuel and Kings are histories. Job, Ecclesiastes, and Proverbs are books of wisdom.

So what kind of book is Daniel? That's a complicated question. Daniel will likely be found in the Bible with the Prophets, after Ezekiel and before the twelve Minor Prophets; and most people treat the book as if it belongs to that genre. But in the Jewish Bible you'll find Daniel neither in the Law or Prophets, but in what is called the Writings, a catch-all category that includes poetry, story, and wisdom. Though the Book of Daniel resembles the Prophets in some superficial ways, our Jewish ancestors recognized that Daniel, especially the second half, belongs completely to another genre, or type.

The type of writing in Daniel is called apocalyptic, taken from the Greek word for revelation. Apocalyptic literature was written to encourage God's people when they were under persecution or other types of trials. Sometimes apocalyptic writing seems strange because it was often written in a sort of code. It was written in such a way that persecuted people could read it, understand it, and be comforted without revealing the real message to their persecutors.

There are two types of apocalyptic literature. There are those stories in which a person travels through heavenly places to see things normally inaccessible to people, and there are those that provide a review of history in which evil is ultimately defeated. Apocalyptic stories emphasize the connectedness between heaven and earth and point out that what happens in one realm affects the other.

Apocalyptic stories are told in a style that affects the reader's emotions. The visual images are more powerful than words, and more lasting. And at the heart of this style of story is the assurance that there is judgment waiting for all of God's creation.

Apocalyptic stories are written to assure the oppressed that God is in control of history and will wrap things up in a manner of his choosing. But while they wait for God to act, God's people are to live according to God's rules and not the world's rules. And though apocalyptic stories may look ahead to the end of time, they have an equal concern for the world's present state.

Daniel is only one example of this type of book. The Old Testament also includes the apocalyptic prophecies of Zechariah. In the New Testament there is Revelation and chapters in the Gospels, such as Mark 13. This literature shows in graphic form what is really going on in the universe. It may look like a mess to us, but God has something in store.

Copyright Date
Daniel stories are set in exile, but is that when Daniel was written? Some say it was written not long after the time of the historical Daniel, in the sixth century B.C. But others believe Daniel was written during what is known as the Intertestamental Period, at least four hundred years after the exile. That's because, although events are placed in the period during and right after the Babylonian exile, the issues that Daniel takes on are more closely related to the persecution of Jews under Antiochus IV

Epiphanes in the mid-second century before Christ. Moreover, the language and the historical references come from the period between Malachi and Matthew, the end of the Old Testament and the beginning of the New.

One way of understanding the real meaning of Daniel is to say that the stories of Israelite endurance under the oppressive hand of the Babylonian empire were inspiring to Jews who were persecuted in the second century B.C. And the events of both the exile and the second-century persecution are helpful to us in our times of trial as well, because the book is for all places and all times, not just one place or one time.

In the Book of Daniel, it is Nebuchadnezzar, the Babylonian king, who persecutes the Israelites. But the visions also point in a thinly veiled way to Antiochus IV Epiphanes, who ruled Syria from 175-164 B.C. His name means "God Revealed," which the Jews considered downright blasphemous. His mission was to spread Greek culture throughout the world, even at the expense of local religions. He wanted his gods to be first, and he attempted to stamp out everything that set our Jewish brothers and sisters apart from their neighbors, which is what Daniel and his companions are experiencing in chapter 1.

Another telltale feature is that a portion of Daniel is written in Aramaic, the common language of the ancient world in the second century. This was one good way for the message about the God of Israel to go out to all people. That it was written in Aramaic leads scholars to think the Book of Daniel was written around 165 B.C.

It may seem strange that a book written in 165 B.C. would sound as if it were written in 530 B.C., but that is normal for this type of story in the Bible. Just as Negro spirituals in the form of church hymns and folktales disguised the slaves' desire for freedom and allowed slaves to laugh at how stupid their masters were, so too people could laugh at Antiochus IV Epiphanes as long as it looked like they were laughing at a long dead Nebuchadnezzar. It is in effect a backward look to the days of Daniel and the terrible times in which he lived, in order to give encouragement to those who were suffering in the present terrible time.

What's in There?

Regardless of when the book was actually written down, many of the stories are very old. They are part of a rich oral tradition, which a second-century-B.C. writer compiled into a book long after the stories were first told. The stories of the first six chapters of Daniel are set in the Babylonian exile. They are the ones most familiar to us from our childhoods—Daniel in the Lion's Den, the Three Young Men in the Fiery Furnace, and the Handwriting on the Wall.

The last six chapters contain four elaborate visions, and it is this section that either puzzles readers or convinces them that they alone know the future. In reality, these chapters tell the very same message as the first six, but in a different format. They are apocalyptic. And the message is not that the world as we know it is coming to an end, or that the world is headed for a cataclysmic battle. The message is that God is in control of history and if we hold on, we will enjoy the blessings of God's plan for the world. But hold on we must, because trial is unavoidable. As it says in the poem *Desiderata*, "And whether or not it is clear to you, no doubt the universe is unfolding as it should."

Discussion and Action

1. Tell about a time in your life when you needed endurance. How did you know if the end was in sight or if the situation would go on indefinitely? What difference did it make to know whether or not the end was in sight?

2. Think of the people you know who are enduring an endless burden, such as caring for someone or suffering from a disease. How can you be supportive to them when the burden is more than they can bear? Consider giving support as a covenant group to someone who needs it. For instance, take in meals, provide transportation, and give a caregiver a rest break.

3. What is the difference between accepting your lot in life and enduring? Which did Daniel do? How? Suppose your community was under siege. What action would you take?

4. Does faithfulness guarantee our rescue from tough times? Why or why not?

5. What are the consequences of being faithful in our culture? What are the rewards? List the marks of your faithfulness. That is, how can others in the community see how you are being faithful. Commit yourselves to displaying the signs of faith more clearly to others. For example, volunteer time with agencies or people who need help, make financial gifts to service and mission work of the church, or live more simply.

6. Remaining chapters suggest two readings a week, one from Daniel and one from the Apocrypha. Make sure that Bibles with the Apocrypha are available to all.

2

Speaking the Truth, No Matter What
Daniel 2; Judith 8

When the king asks Daniel to interpret his very peculiar dream, Daniel has to decide whether to tell the king what he wants to hear or what God says the dream means.

Personal Preparation

1. Read Daniel 2 and Judith 8. As you read, look for ways in which the stories are similar and ways they are different. Both Daniel and Judith resist the temptation to test God. Have you ever tested God? How?
2. Call to mind a vivid dream. How did the dream inspire you or warn you? Keep track of your dreams this week. What are they telling you?
3. The dream in Daniel 2 is about speaking the truth to power. Begin a list of people in Bible times and since, including people you know today, who have spoken the truth to power.

Understanding

Dreams are important even if we don't remember them. It's one way the mind has of sorting through the memory, keeping some things and disposing of a lot of odds and ends. It is a way for our subconscious to speak to us and let us know what we're really concerned about. Dreams can even be a source of prophecy.

I remember a particularly vivid dream I had when I was in the sixth grade. It had to do with a fire consuming a building on the shoreline of the sea and people escaping by boat. Perhaps escape is not the right word. The boat was sailing across the sea to heaven. The journey would take a little while so that people had time to prepare for glory. The day before the ship was to land on the distant shore, a picture of Jesus appeared in the cabin of one of the voyagers.

It was a wonderful dream. I was sad to wake up from it, but I was also filled with the feeling that this was a gift. Before this dream I had had many anxieties about death. Afterward they were gone.

But some dreams are just the opposite. They terrorize us, and when we wake up we cannot shake off the terror. I'm reminded of a scene in the C. S. Lewis book *The Voyage of the Dawn Treader*. Like my dream, it is about a ship on its way to the very edge of heaven. At one point the mariners rescue a haggard man from a mysterious island, a place, he explains, where dreams come true.

At first the sailors think they would like to stay where dreams come true, until the haggard man explains that he's not talking about daydreams, but real dreams. As each sailor calls to mind the horrible nightmares he's had and what it would be like to live in such a place, they row away with renewed purpose. No one wants to live in a place where those kinds of dreams come to life.

Nightmare in Babylon

In chapter 2 of Daniel, King Nebuchadnezzer has a nightmare. The horror remains with him even after he is fully awake. The dream is so bad even he, the mightiest ruler on the earth, is reduced to a whimpering child. What does this dream mean? He calls on the people who are supposed to know about these things—"the magicians, the enchanters, the sorcerers, and the Chaldeans."

In the ancient world, there were dream books, books that listed all kinds of dreams and what they meant. Babylonian interpreters could have given a stock answer to the king's questions by consulting their books if they were told the dream. Nebuchadnezzar knows this, but he doesn't want a pat answer based on a handbook. The king makes an extraordinary demand. He commands that the interpreters demonstrate their skill by telling him not only what his dream means, but what his dream was. The reward, if they succeed—great gifts! And if they fail— "to be torn limb from limb, and [their] houses shall be laid in ruins" (2:5). Do the impossible or die.

His counselors level with him. "There is no one on earth who can reveal what the king demands!" (2:10). In fact, no king, however great and powerful, has ever asked such a thing of any magician or enchanter or Chaldean. Only the gods can know the contents of the dream.

They're both right and wrong. The thing the king asks *is* too diffi-cult—for humans. But God's dwelling place is here with us. And there happens to be a person who serves the living God who can help them. Daniel to the rescue!

Daniel and his three companions, as members of the court, are just as likely to be put to death as the astrologers. So with nothing to lose, Daniel approaches the chief executioner, gets the straight story, and asks the official for permission to approach the king. Daniel, the example of virtuosity, volunteers to reveal and interpret the king's dream.

The task is no more possible for Daniel than for any of the astrolo-gers, but Daniel has something they do not have—fellow-believers. He is no lone gun, striding into town at high noon to solve the problem by himself. He belongs to a body of believers, and believers come together to pray. The four gather to pray for God's light, and in the middle of the night the mystery is revealed to Daniel. He responds with a poem of praise, acknowledging that it is really God who is in control of the world. It is God who reveals the truth, not soothsayers.

Typical of apocalyptic stories, something is about to be revealed. The purpose of the story is not to mystify people or speak in a code that only the spiritual elite can figure out. It is to reveal the truth. We know that the basic truth of Daniel is for everybody, because at the end of Daniel 7, the language of the book shifts from Hebrew to Aramaic, which, during the second century before Christ, was the business language of the world, known by commoners and rich alike. Rather than being ob-scured in an archaic language read only by a small group of people in an out-of-the-way province, the message of God's sovereignty over his-tory is presented in a language most people could understand.

When Daniel appears before the great king, he is careful to give God the credit for the mystery he is about to reveal. But while Daniel shows proper respect to God, he is still doing a very risky thing—he dares to say to the king that the God of the conquered Jews is more powerful than the conquering king himself. But Daniel has a powerful weapon to protect him. The truth. God's truth has revealed the king's dream.

Daniel tells it like it is. Nebuchadnezzar has seen a great statue of enormous size. The head was gold, the chest and arms silver, its middle and thighs bronze, legs of iron, and feet part iron and part clay. Out of nowhere a great stone appeared, breaking the statue at the feet and caus-ing the whole structure to collapse.

This particular statue symbolizes the four stages of an empire as was understood by the Jews around the time of the Maccabees. Nebuchadnezzar's empire was golden, the empire of the Medes was silver, the Persian empire was bronze, and the Greek empire, personified by Alexander the Great, was iron. Though bronze and iron are not valuable metals, they are still strong. No matter how well a structure is built, however, it is only as strong as its weakest portion. And when a mysterious stone strikes the clay feet, the statue crumbles.

The feet of the statue represent the fragmentation of Alexander's great realm after his death, when the empire was divided among his four generals. The clay portion of the feet may represent Antiochus IV Epiphanes.

The stone, which then becomes a mountain, is God's eternal kingdom, which will outlast the other kingdoms. The central message of the dream is clear. In God's time his kingdom will appear and these earthly kingdoms shall pass away.

After Me, the Flood

In the meantime Nebuchadnezzer seems to be confident that at least for his lifetime his kingdom will endure. Perhaps you've heard the French expression *Apres moi, le deluge*—After me, the flood. That is, let the oil run out after my life, let the rainforests last throughout my days, let the ozone layer hold out a little longer; that's the attitude of the shortsighted. Nebuchadnezzar will be surprised.

When the stories of Daniel first appeared as a book, scripture scholars wove elaborate schemes to explain the dream further. Early Christians rearranged it to include Rome as the fourth empire. Others have seen Islam, the Holy Roman Empire, the Soviet Union, and any proposed European union as the feet of clay. They're all wrong. And right. It's a waste of time to worry about which empire is which part of the statue. If we live in broken times, we live in the fourth empire.

Some Christians believe the stone represents Christ. He is the one who is more powerful than empires, who outlasts kingdoms, who rules and reigns today. Whether we interpret the stone as God, God's kingdom, or Christ, the dream still works. God is in control, and the kingdoms of the world are ultimately powerless. Earthly kingdoms last for a day. But in the days to come, "the God of heaven will set up a kingdom that shall never be destroyed" (2:44a).

Daniel speaks truth to power with the executioner waiting in the wings, and what Daniel gets for speaking up is not punishment, but a reward. Nebuchadnezzar promotes him to rule over the city of Babylon. The important point, however, is that Daniel acted faithfully not knowing the outcome. To act only on assurances is not faith.

The Apocrypha

The Apocrypha is a group of books unfamiliar to many Christians. Written by God's people during what is known as the Intertestamental Period, the time between the last of the minor prophets and the beginning of New Testament, these books were not chosen to be part of the Bible as we know it today. However, most of them are accepted as scripture by the Roman Catholic and Eastern Orthodox Churches. Other Christian groups, including some Protestant denominations, include these books in a separate section between the Old and New Testaments and refer to them as Deuterocanonical, meaning the "second canon."

The history of how the books of the Bible came to be chosen over other holy writings is long, complicated, and controversial. In short, for centuries scripture consisted of scholarly Latin translations of the Greek and Hebrew originals. Of course, ordinary people didn't read the Bible. They didn't read at all, especially Latin. So the meaning of the Bible was interpreted through a trained and sometimes entrenched clergy. With the Reformation, Christians desired to translate the Bible into the language of the people. That's when translators such as Martin Luther noticed that the Hebrew Bible included fewer books than the Latin Bibles. When Reformation translators adopted the same books held sacred by the Jews, the books now relegated to the Apocrypha were eliminated.

Until the present century, these books were printed in a separate section of the Bible but were accepted by all Christians as profitable for reading, if not for doctrinal use. Samples of these books are included in this study because many stem from roughly the same period of history and complement or contrast the views expressed in the Book of Daniel.

Enter Judith

The Book of Judith is a good example of both the Apocrypha and apocalyptic writing. It is apocalyptic in the sense that God reveals a plan of hope to a people living under persecution. And as a book of the Apocrypha, it sounds a lot like actual scripture, especially some of the scriptural histories. Even though the facts in Judith are a little mixed up, the beginning of Judith sounds like sober history: "It was in the twelfth year of the reign of Nebuchadnezzar, who ruled over the Assyrians in the great city of Ninevah" (1:1). But the great king ruled over the Babylonians, not the Assyrians, and the persecution more closely resembles that of an even later era. It is as if someone were writing about George Washington and Abraham Lincoln joining Martin Luther King, Jr., on the march on Washington in 1963. And the geography is just as confused as the history.

But it doesn't matter. Indeed, some think the writer deliberately confuses the facts so readers will focus on the story instead of the history. The intent is to display the power of God to deliver his people. A great army led by the Assyrian Holofernes is poised against a small town of Israelites called Bethulia. There seems to be no escape for God's people. The situation is impossible. A deadline is set. Bethulia gives God five days to deliver them or they will surrender.

The first seven chapters of the book are pretty boring. But enter Judith in the eighth chapter. Suddenly the story picks up. This pious, beautiful, and rich widow of Bethulia challenges the leaders of her people, saying, "Who are you to put God to the test today? (8:12)." Like Daniel, Judith refuses to base her faith in God on whether or not God will bail them out. A woman with few legal rights in her day dares to speak this truth to the powerful Hebrews who have lost faith in God. After chastising her people, she declares that, as one who trusts in God, she herself will deliver her people. And she does.

With only her maidservant to aid her, Judith traps the great and mighty conqueror Holofernes (probably a Persian general who lived around the year 350 B.C.) with her beauty. He thinks he'll seduce her, and Judith leads him on. But when he's asleep, she cuts off his head and stuffs it in a sack. Judith escapes and returns to her people.

The next day, when his army discovers that Holofernes is dead, they flee in all directions. Judith is recognized as a great hero, and God is glorified through her actions. Like Daniel, Judith gives the credit to God. And like Nebuchadnezzar in the second chapter of Daniel, a Gentile named Achior acknowledges the power of the Hebrew God (Judith 14:10). In fact, Achior had warned Holofernes about attacking the Jews whose God was supreme, but when he did, Holofernes drove him away, threatening Achior with a terrible fate when the Israelites were conquered.

Some treat the second chapter of Daniel as a description of the end of time, but the phrase "end of days" merely refers to human history, whose kingdoms come and go. But the kingdom of God is always ahead. Both Judith and Daniel speak this truth not because they have special knowledge of it, but because God used them to reveal it to us all. The message of both gives us hope for our day, not just the future.

Discussion and Action

1. Daniel and Judith remind us that God is in control of the world. What evidence do you see that God is in control? Tell about ways you have tested God's control. For instance, have you

ever promised to live faithfully if God will save you from some situation? How did it work out?

2. If you were able to add or subtract books of the Bible, which would they be? Why? As a group, make a list of your favorite books of the Bible. As a whole, what do these books say about you?

3. What do you think of the books of the Apocrypha? Do they have authority for your life? Why or why not?

4. Recount to each other your dreams of this past week. Try your hand at interpreting them. Is God trying to say anything to you through your dreams? If your group is large, divide into smaller groups so everyone has a chance to contribute.

5. Daniel brought together his brothers in the faith to pray for insight. What part do members of your covenant group or people in your congregation play in helping to understand God's plan for us?

6. Both Daniel and Judith spoke the truth to powerful leaders. Where do we need to speak the truth to powers today? To the principal, to one's boss, to city hall? Who are the powers? Are powers always evil? What needs to be said to powers today? Consider writing letters to members of Congress or the president about an issue that concerns you.

7. J. Robert Oppenheimer tried to tell President Truman of the dangers of the atomic bomb, but government leaders would not listen. How is the church called to expose false prophecy, false gods?
   Share your list of people who have spoken the truth to the powers of their day.

8. The truth spoken by Nelson Mandela of South Africa was eventually heard in his country, but the truth spoken by the Chinese students in Tiananmen Square has not been heard by the powers. Was their witness in vain? How long should they endure? How do you define success?

3

Faithful, No Matter What
Daniel 3; 2 Maccabees 7

Shadrach, Meshach, and Abednego submit themselves to the fiery furnace willingly. They don't do it for the rewards. They do it because it is the faithful thing to do. As the Maccabee family knows, faith is not always rewarded with blessings. Sometimes faith brings death. Is faith worth it?

Personal Preparation

1. Read Daniel 3 and 2 Maccabees 7. As you read, recall areas of the world today that are suffering under oppression and war. Imagine the risks Christians are taking to be faithful. Pray for the strength to be faithful under pressure.

2. When have you, or someone you know, chosen faithfulness over the dictates of government, society, or powerful leaders? How did others treat you or this person at the time and after?

3. In your view, do civic duty and Christian faith go together? Jesus said, "Render to Caesar the things that are Caesar's, and to God the things that are God's" (Mark 12:17 RSV). What do you give to Caesar and what do you give to God? Do they ever conflict? In what way?

Understanding

Children—and adults—enjoy repetition in their stories, like when the big bad wolf says, "I'll huff and I'll puff and I'll blow your house down." Or when the gingerbread man says, "Run, run, run, just as fast you can. You can't catch me. I'm the gingerbread man."

Repetition is fun and funny. It also makes stories easier to tell and remember. If you've ever told stories or read books to children, you know how they demand that you use the same phrases over and over again. Whenever I told the story of the *Three Billy Goats Gruff* to nursery school children, I always had to describe the troll exactly the same way each time he made an appearance. If I didn't, the children would correct me.

The third chapter of Daniel uses this technique of repetition with great humor. Nebuchadnezzar sets up a statue and calls "the satraps, the prefects, and the governors, the counselors, the treasurers, the justices, the magistrates, and all the officials of the provinces to assemble and come to the dedication of the statue" (3:2). Instead of simply saying that all those guys obeyed, the next verse reads "So the satraps, the prefects, and the governors, the counselors, the treasurers, the justices, the magistrates, and all the officials of the provinces, assembled for the dedication of the statue that King Nebuchadnezzar had set up" (3:3).

The signal for the people to fall down and worship the statue is also a repetitive phrase. When the people "hear the sound of the horn, pipe, lyre, trigon, harp, drum, and entire musical ensemble, you are to fall down and worship the golden statue that King Nebuchadnezzar has set up" (3:5.) The penalty for failure to comply is fierce. Those who do not bow down will be thrown into a fiery furnace.

Sure enough, two verses later, the people hear the sound "of the horn, pipe, lyre, trigon, harp, drum, and entire musical ensemble" (3:7), and all bow down. It's almost impossible not to think of slapstick comedians when the satraps, the prefects, and the governors, the counselors, the treasurers, the justices, the magistrates, and all the officials of the provinces trip over each other to fall down first at the sound of the horn, pipe, lyre, trigon, harp, drum, and entire musical ensemble. BLAT! go the instruments. Drop go the loyal subjects. Except for three people whose names provide that beautifully repeated set of syllables, "Shadrach, Meshach, and Abednego." Try saying that several times.

These three young men were introduced as the companions of Daniel in the first chapter. Just as they chose not to eat at the king's table when doing so meant breaking Jewish law, these three servants of the one God, Yahweh, are not about to comply with a request to bow down and worship an inanimate object.

How Far Can We Go?

This story presents one of the central dilemmas for the believer. To what extent can we participate in the life of the state? To what extent are we a people apart, separate from the un-Christian things a government does? The answer varies depending on the time and circumstance. Daniel and the three young men are men of faith, but they are also highly respected court officials. They loyally serve the conquering king because they believe their own Israel's defeat was the result of its unfaithfulness, and they are doing penance. Even Jesus suggested that we have some duty to the state when he ordered his critics to render to Caesar the things that are Caesar's, and to God the things that are God's.

But there are limits. At first glance the state's demand to worship the statue is reasonable. Nebuchadnezzar does not tell the three young men to abandon their faith, nor is he attempting to eradicate their religion. He says in effect, "You may worship and pray as you choose, but you must add this single duty as well."

In the end, however, the Book of Daniel tells us we cannot serve God and country if it means putting country on an equal basis with God. We are perfectly free to serve the state as long as we put God first. In other words, you cannot add worship of the state to the worship of God.

During times of national crisis, there is pressure to put our faith second, to perform acts as individuals and nations that we would consider immoral under other circumstances. Some people equate Christianity and patriotism as one and the same. Daniel would disagree.

The fact that the young men are in the town square at the time of this incident is natural, as they are court officials. Thus, their disobedience is public. Since Daniel and his companions have come up through the ranks so quickly, surpassing native Chaldeans, their fellow courtiers are jealous. That is part of the reason they blow the whistle on Shadrach, Meshach, and Abednego—again going through the catalog of musical instruments. The Chaldeans despise the men and are quick to rat on them, reminding Nebuchadnezzar that "there are certain Jews whom you have appointed over the affairs of the province of Babylon. . . . These pay no heed to you" (3:12).

This jealousy has been a consistent part of the Jewish experience. Jews who have been successful financially, intellectually, and other ways have often come up against jealous resistance from others. They are often stereotyped as shrewd and crafty business people, snobbish academics, pushy and arrogant citizens who barely have a right to live in "our" society.

Only in recent decades have churches begun to confess their sins of intolerance for others. The confessing churches in Germany have admitted their silence that contributed to the murder of millions of Jews and others during World War II. In America churches have begun to confess that they participated in racial segregation and oppression and even hindered the civil rights process.

The Defense Rests

When the three young men are brought before the king, they say nothing instead of rallying to their own defense, which is what we would want to do if accused: "O Nebuchadnezzar, we have no need to present a defense to you in this matter. If our God whom we serve is able to deliver us from the furnace of blazing fire and out of your hand, O king, let him deliver us. But if not, be it known to you, O king, that we will not serve your gods and we will not worship the golden statue that you have set up" (3:16-18). That's it.

Note that in the first sentence the young men do not use the king's title when they address him. It is another reminder of their priorities.

More importantly, the young men make it clear that their God is capable of rescuing them, but even if God chooses not to, they will not bow down. God's claim on their loyalty is greater than the threat of death.

Just as the adversary in Job suggested that Job only honored God to receive blessings, we might have wondered up to this point if these three very devout men were just "goody two shoes," looking for an "in" with God. But by their willingness to risk death without assurances of being saved, the three young men prove their faith is not merely based upon what God can do for them.

Deliverance

So enraged is the king that he not only commands the three offenders to be thrown into the fiery kiln, he also orders that it be heated to seven times its usual temperature. So urgent is his rage that the three young men are thrown into the kiln fully clothed, even though it was customary in the ancient world to strip the condemned before execution. The fire is so hot it kills even the executioners as they approach the furnace.

To the king's astonishment, when he looks through a door in the kiln, he sees four figures walking unharmed in the midst of the flames. We can't know from the text who the fourth person is, though there has been a lot of speculation. Later Jewish tradition identifies this fourth figure as an angel, according to an apocryphal addition to the story called the Prayer of Azariah (the Hebrew name of Abednego): "But the angel of the Lord came down into the furnace to be with Azariah and his companions, and drove the flame out of the furnace, and made the inside of the furnace as though a moist wind were whistling through it. The fire did not touch them at all and caused them no pain or distress" (Azariah 26-27). The only casualties of the fire were the ropes that bound them.

When the king calls Meschach, Shadrach, and Abednego out of the furnace, he addresses them with respect as servants of God Most High, which is what Gentiles called God. Nebuchadnezzar issues a decree that no one is to utter a blasphemy against this God Most High. It is all coming clear to Nebuchadnezzar now. In the second chapter of Daniel, he learns that God reveals; in the third chapter he sees that God acts directly in history.

The crucial point is that the three were not saved *from* the fire, but *in* the fire. It's important to remember that sometimes God brings deliverance in the midst of our trials, but he does not deliver us from them. "When you pass through the waters, I will be with you; and through the rivers, they shall not overwhelm you; when you walk through fire you shall not be burned, and the flame shall not consume you" (Isa. 43:2).

Heroes

When I was in high school, George Orwell's novel *1984* was required reading. This pessimistic book claims that totalitarianism will triumph because there are no heroes in the face of pain. My religious background told me this was patently false, however. From the stories of martyrs, which I heard as a child, I knew that people could be very heroic. Though it seemed to me that no one wanted to be a martyr, those stories made it clear that when many of our mothers and fathers in the faith faced torture and death, they remained faithful.

In our own era, I think of the people who found themselves facing dangerous circumstances and did the faithful thing in spite of the danger—the Corrie Ten Booms who harbored Jews from the Nazis, the Martin Luther Kings who confronted racial discrimination, the church people who reached out to interned Japanese Americans, and those who went to prison rather than go against the biblical injunction not to kill, even if in the military. Each of us can name brave people we know who have been heroes in the faith.

The ancient stories of martyrs and the contemporary stories of faith are a way of saying Hold on! Beyond the pain is his eternal glory. What at the moment seems like abandonment is really the ultimate success. As Paul's letter to the Romans says, "If we live, we live to the Lord, and if we die, we die to the Lord; so then, whether we live or whether we die, we are the Lord's" (Rom. 14:8).

The story of the three young men in the furnace has been a great inspiration to many throughout the history of the faithful. One of the most popular designs on tombstones in the catacombs shows the story of the three young men in the fiery furnace. It was the Christians' touch-

stone, the proof of a pure faith. After he had suffered great torture because of his faith and before he was burned at the stake in 1572,
Anabaptist martyr Jan Woutersz van Cuyck wrote, "Rather go with Daniel
in the lions' den than that I should kneel down before wood, stone, gold,
silver, bread, wine, or oil. Rather go with the young men in the fiery
furnace, than worship the image, which was set up."

It is not always the case, however, that the faithful are delivered from
the furnace. Some have displayed the same faith as the heroes of this
tale, but suffered death and not physical deliverance. One of the most
famous of these stories comes from 2 Maccabees 7. First Maccabees
professes to be a straight history of the Greek ruler Antiochus Epiphanes
and the Maccabee family. While based on a true story, 2 Maccabees
emphasizes the theological side of history—not what happened, but an
interpretation of what events mean for God's people. In the same way, 1
and 2 Chronicles interprets the events of Samuel and Kings. The heroes
in 2 Maccabees look ahead to God's vindication and eternal life.

In the horrible story in chapter 7, a mother and her seven sons are
executed one by one in front of each other, each professing his faith and
refusing to eat pork from pagan sacrifices to satisfy a foreign king. It is
not certain that the individuals who suffered spoke the exact words attributed to them. In martyrologies (stories of martyrs), speeches were
fashioned by recorders to make clear the important points of what the
deaths signified. That the seven brothers and their mother strengthened
each other through their words and that they openly defied the king
cannot be doubted, however.

Believers of that time knew they could not always expect or demand to be delivered like Meschach, Shadrach, and Abednego, for
experience told them otherwise. They also would have known the
story of 2 Maccabees 7, the case of a family who was not delivered
even though they were faithful under horrible persecution. In that
day the Maccabees' example was just as important to God's people
as the story of the three young men.

It is interesting to note that while atrocities were common throughout ancient history, the first recorded persecution on the basis of religion alone was that of Antiochus IV Epiphanes against the Jewish people,
recorded in 1 and 2 Maccabees. The stories of Daniel had strong meaning for those enduring persecution under Antiochus. Hold on!

Today our faith is also tested in the fiery furnace of our lives. Like
Jesus and the martyrs of the church, we do not seek to escape the test,
for it could be said that untested faith is no faith at all. Trust in God is an
essential ingredient in surviving life's torments. Once we know and be-

lieve we are connected to heaven, that history has a higher purpose. Once we see this moment in a larger context, we see things differently; and how we see things changes how we experience things. Deliverance, salvation, and faith become radically new concepts, energizing us to do the will of God.

In the end the story proves that the threats of a king are no threats at all. There is a real God, and this God acts in history.

Discussion and Action

1. Who was with the three men in the furnace? Who is with you in trial?
2. What fiery furnaces have you endured? Which have you avoided? Has such "testing" served a purpose? Or does it seem to you totally senseless?
3. The three young men in Daniel were delivered, but the seven sons in 2 Maccabees 7 were not. What forms does deliverance take in our lives today? For what reasons might God not deliver someone?
4. Like Daniel and the Maccabees, what are your limits with the government? Is there any clear guide to how much you can cooperate with the government? Does it make a difference if the state or government is friendly or unfriendly to the faith? To what extent does the state function on God's behalf?
5. Compare your limits at the local, state/province, and national levels. Do you set different limits at each level?
6. What counsel does your church or denomination give on Christian participation with government?
7. What long-term effects does martyrdom have? If it seems pointless in the short run, how effective is it in the long run? Consider people like Anne Frank, Joan of Arc, Martin Luther King, Jr., Jesus.

4

Hearing the Truth
Daniel 4; 1 Esdras 3–4

When the king asks Daniel to interpret a dream, he has to hear the unpleasant truth that there is a greater king than he. His bad news is our good news: over all rulers is one king, God Most High, who is greater than any earthly ruler or power.

Personal Preparation

1. Read Daniel 4 and 1 Esdras 3–4. Have you ever had to listen to someone tell you an unpleasant truth about yourself? How did you react? What happened to the relationship?
2. Whose authority do you respect most in life? That of a friend? your spouse? a pastor? the Bible? God? If any of these were to judge you, how would you take it?
3. When you are truthful with others, how do you phrase your criticism so they will accept it? When is bare honesty necessary?
4. Like the courtiers in Esdras 3–4, think this week about what is greatest in your life. Write down your reasons.

Understanding

Most years our family makes a trek to southern Oregon where my in-laws live. We always time our visit to coincide with the Oregon Shakespeare Festival in Ashland, which has the largest repertory theater in the United States. Some seventy actors, four hundred technicians, and eight hundred volunteers put on twelve shows, as many as nine simultaneously, from February through October.

Of all the plays I have watched, the one with the most striking set was the 1987 production of *Richard II*. Behind a series of towers and turrets was a giant circle, representing the "wheel of fortune" of Greek philosophy (not the game show). As the wheel turned, the fortunes of different families rose or fell. It was a graphic demonstration of an idea that was popular for centuries and understood all too well by the Elizabethans who first saw the play. Simply put, everyone, no matter how great or obscure, could expect times of good or bad fortune. No one was guaranteed good times for every day of their life. No amount of good or bad behavior could change the natural rhythm of life. Today, however, some of us think good fortune is our natural right.

I remember a man who for the first eighty-four years of his life experienced good health and, because he was a hard worker, was able to live pretty much as he pleased. In the last three years of his life, however, he experienced poor health, diminished eyesight, and loss of independence. He became outraged and angry! Why should he have to go through times of difficulty? It wasn't fair. Hadn't he been good? His friends tried to console him, suggesting that these things sometimes occur late in life. They reminded him of his relative good fortune most of his days. But their consolation was all for naught. He would not hear what was said to him.

This man is not alone in believing that his good fortune is the direct result of being good, that in some way he deserves good health and a fat bank account. People who believe this are only hearing the message they want to hear, a message that is nowhere written in the book of nature or the scriptures.

Conversely, I have known families who have experienced misfortune all the days of their lives, far beyond what is fair. Some of them remained faithful to God regardless of what happened. They were able to hear God's voice in the midst of the storm and knew that God was not the storm itself.

Big Mistake

In Daniel 4 the mighty emperor Nebuchadnezzar tells how he falsely believed his good fortune and great power were the direct result of something godlike within himself. Then something happened to cause him to change his mind and recognize that the true God is over him, not in him. In this chapter he writes a letter to the world to affirm that the God of Israel is this God Most High.

Once again Nebuchadnezzar has had a troubling dream. Once again "the magicians, the enchanters, the Chaldeans, and the diviners" (4:7) are unable to interpret the dream. And once again it falls to resident alien Daniel, who is called Belteshazzar, to explain God's mind to the emperor. Not accidently, Daniel's Babylonian name calls to mind the emperor's god (4:8), but Daniel proves that his God is more powerful.

The dream is about a tree that symbolizes the king and his relationship to the entire interdependent cosmos. We have seen this image of the emperor or empire as a tree elsewhere in the Bible. In Ezekiel 31, for instance, a pharaoh is compared to a cedar of Lebanon, and in Ezekiel 17:1-10 the house of David is compared to a tree. Isaiah refers to David's line as the "stump of Jesse." It's an apt image, since the birds of the air and the beasts of the field are sheltered and nourished by trees. A ruler is also expected to shelter and nourish the people. Though it may seem like rulers did nothing but exploit their subjects, in reality they gained the cooperation of the people by providing protection.

The dream forewarns Nebuchadnezzar that he will be stricken down and lose his wits because of his sins. He will lose his self-awareness and act like an animal for seven years, until his wits are restored.

It's not the sort of message one would like to give a king, but Daniel, despite his fears, gives the ruler a most precious gift—the truth. The question is whether the king will hear that truth.

Some believe these stories in the first six chapters of Daniel display a high view of constituted authority. It seems that in instances where it is at all possible Daniel shows respect to earthly leaders. Interestingly, this has been the basis for some Christians, from Augustine to the present, for doing whatever the state requires, regardless of how it conflicts with their faith.

It is important, however, to see that Daniel does not equate kings and God. It is the state's obligation to conform to God's vision of justice and righteousness, not the church's obligation to bless the excesses of governments as some sort of obscure manifestation of God's will.

Many people in high places surround themselves with those who flatter them and drive away those who tell them no. Vidkun Quisling, a Norwegian politician, earned himself a place in history for fawning on the Nazis during World War II and betraying his own people. Flatterers today are called quislings. But Daniel is no such yes man. Though distressed by the message he has to give, he doesn't hesitate to give the king the bad news that a fall is coming.

Daniel does more than tell the truth, which in and of itself is pretty brutal. He displays what Lederach calls a "pastoral heart." He tells the truth without vindictiveness and does not suggest that doom must fall on the emperor. Daniel cares, and he calls on Nebuchadnezzar to change his ways and avert the fate that is foretold.

Not Yet, but Soon

When the exile is delayed, Nebuchadnezzar has a chance to change his ways. Bible scholar Graydon Snyder points out that in scripture virtually all predictions of the Day of the Lord, or a day of doom, have a delay clause. There is time for people to change their ways. That most powerful of words—*if*—was offered as an out. If we do not change our ways, then doom will fall. This is an offer of hope.

There is also the warning that God's patience will not last forever. Sooner or later time will run out. But true to human nature, we often ignore the warning signs. For example, God's people had ample warning over the centuries to be more faithful, but they continued to disobey and were finally conquered and led away into exile.

In our own lives, it is important that we both tell the truth and hear the truth. A doctor may tell us that if we cut out salt, or fat, or sugar, we can restore our health. We have to change our behavior or else! When we don't, a loved one may adopt the courage of Daniel to tell us the truth. If no one tells the truth and no one hears the truth, the consequence may be as final as death.

Sometimes we just don't want to hear the warning. I remember a prophetic dream told me by my wife, Jennie. We were in seminary in Illinois and expecting our first child two months after graduation. Then our plan was to return to our native California.

In the weeks before I graduated, however, Jennie had a dream that when our first child was born, we wouldn't have any clothes for him and he would have to sleep in a drawer. I told her the idea was silly. Sure enough, when Francisco was born three months early, we had not yet purchased any clothes for him, and between the time of his release from the hospital and our move to California, he had to sleep in a drawer.

They'll Do It Every Time

The next step seems almost inevitable. A year after the dream, the emperor looks out over his fabled palace. The palace included large courtyards, a throne room, opulent bedrooms and reception areas, as well as the famous hanging gardens, which were watered by an ingenious watering system. The hanging gardens of Babylon are still known as one of the seven wonders of the ancient world. And all this was just the center of a larger series of walls, gates, temples, squares, and statuary.

But when Nebuchadnezzar says, "Is this not magnificent Babylon, which I have built as a royal capital by my mighty power and for my glorious majesty?" (4:30), the gift of consciousness is taken away, and he lives and acts like a beast for seven years. Nebuchadnezzar has taken all the credit for himself. He has not heeded the warnings. In consequence, Babel comes to Babylon. The gift of speech and reason is taken away for having been abused.

Fortunately for Nebuchadnezzar, it is not God's aim to destroy, but to restore recognition of the true sovereign. After a period of seven years, reason is restored to the king, who responds by praising the God Most High. As long as the king acknowledges that there is one who is more powerful, there is hope and a happy ending. Wisdom triumphs. Even a king can be cured.

There is something comic about the story, the image of the great king eating grass, his hair and nails growing grotesquely long. It's unlikely that a mighty emperor would write a letter as described here, and historians can't identify seven missing years in the forty-three-year reign of Nebuchadnezzar, although there are legends of madness associated with emperors in the ancient world.

The story calls to mind the *Narnia Chronicles*, by C. S. Lewis. In this fantasy series, children from our world discover a way into a land called Narnia, where the Lord is a lion, and the beasts can speak. The gift of consciousness is solemnly given to the animals by the lion at the creation, and in the final book of the series, *The Last Battle*, some lose that as well.

The Babylonians considered their kingdom the gate of heaven. In the story of the Tower of Babel, however, human pride in accomplishment was punished by being stripped of one of the most human distinctives—language. Far from being the gate of heaven, Babylon had become the home of babble, a pun that works as well in Hebrew as in English.

In our day it is unlikely we would put our faith in a physical building, but we have built a new Tower of Babel in replacing faith with science. Science in itself is a good thing. We live longer and better because of the advances in scientific knowledge. Much backbreaking physical labor has been replaced by machines produced by science. Some diseases have been eradicated.

But all these advances are based on possibilities inherent in God's creation, and when we take the sole credit without praising the Creator, we become like Nebuchadnezzar in this story. Rather than praising God as the source of all wisdom and authority, some scientists (and some sociologists and some theologians, for that matter) adopt the attitude that we are somehow high priests of knowledge that belongs solely to us. We wrap our words in an unintelligible jargon that is an affront to the gift of the Spirit and the foundation of a new and even more terrifying Tower of Babel—the ability and inclination to say absolutely nothing in a manner that impresses otherwise sensible people. That is our modern Babel.

There is also something comic about this story. Apocalyptic stories often include judgment on the high, who are then brought low. Those who first heard this tale would have laughed to imagine the great and mighty Nebuchadnezzar lowered to the state of a beast. The wheel of fortune turns both up and down for the emperor.

Like many of the stories in Daniel, this one fits into what scholars call "the court tale." In this type of story, rulers are often duped by dishonest ministers, but truth always triumphs, and they are rescued by someone humble but honest. *The Emperor's New Clothes* is an example of this type of story. Joseph's interpretation of Pharaoh's dream and his subsequent rise from prisoner to administrator is another good example.

According to Bible scholar John J. Collins, author of a commentary on Daniel, "These tales express a basically optimistic view of the world. Ministers who fall into disgrace can be rehabilitated. Monarchs who act impetuously will eventually see the folly of their ways. . . . the value of wisdom is affirmed. Wise courtiers will succeed, even at the court of an alien king."

Which Is the Greatest?

The tale of the three young men from 1 Esdras is another good example of a court tale. First Esdras, which in some Bibles would be called Third Ezra, includes paraphrases of certain passages in 2 Chronicles, Ezra, and a smattering of Nehemiah. The purpose of this book, possibly written in the period right before the Maccabees, was to place the historical Ezra on an equal plane with Josiah, the last just king of God's people, and Zerubbabel, the first governor of Judah after the return of the exiles. But the purpose of this particular story is purely to delight. We are to hear that there is something greater than wine, song, and kings. It is God's truth.

The story was probably an old one that was altered by the author with a special purpose in mind. Just like Nebuchadnezzar, King Darius has trouble sleeping. Three young bodyguards of the king devise an entertainment for the court. They decide to debate the question, What is the strongest thing? In a brazen move, they determine ahead of time what honors the king should bestow on them for winning.

The three young men place their arguments under the king's pillow. One insists "Wine is strongest." The second believes "The king is strongest." The third, who is revealed to be Zerubbabel, future governor of

Judea, is not afraid to defend his thesis: "Women are strongest, but above all things truth is victor."

In common with this week's story from Daniel, this tale announces that the king is not the strongest and that someone has the courage, like Daniel, to say so. The first debater makes a good case for his thesis that wine is a great leveler. "It makes equal the mind of the king and the orphan, of the slave and the free, of the poor and the rich" (1 Esdras 3:19). The second debater defends a common—and flattering—claim that the king is the strongest.

But Zerubbabel makes a strong case that women rule men and are therefore stronger, but that truth is stronger than them all. He concludes, "Blessed be the God of truth!"

This clever court tale reaffirms that rulers are important, but their place in society is part of a scheme that is larger than themselves. Zerubbabel receives his reward but gives God the credit. The reader of these two stories reacts in delight at seeing either the high brought low or the low brought high. How hard it is to hear the truth, and how blessed to hear a ruler say, "Blessed be the God of truth."

Discussion and Action

1. When we are good, do we or do we not deserve to have good fortune? If we do, how good is good? What are the rewards for good deeds? for better deeds? for the best deeds? Is it possible to judge which deeds deserve which fortunes? Why? Why not?

2. What should our attitude be toward the authorities in our country and the leaders in our governments? Should we be compliant like Daniel? Should we outright object when things go wrong? What kind of respect do you give authorities in your own life?

3. How does our government conform to God's will and God's sense of justice and righteousness? In what ways does the state expect religion to conform to its expectations?

4. How can we, like Daniel, tell the truth without vindictiveness? How can we control our feelings of "I told you so" or our feelings of superiority when we speak truth to power? Name real situations and talk about how you can have a pastoral heart as you confront them.

5. What "out" does God provide to Christians who sin? Is there anything we can do that will make God believe we are worthless? If so, what? What corporate sins can we still correct if we change our ways?

6. Who are the kings and leaders today who have claimed more authority than they are due? Where do we as Christians and citizens need to give God credit rather than giving it to rulers and leaders?

7. What are the limits of knowledge? In what areas will knowledge never help us? How can God help us in these areas?

8. Close with prayer, giving God credit for creation and everything in it.

5

Your Days Are Numbered
Daniel 5; 1 Maccabees 1–2

The handwriting is on the wall. The king's days are numbered. The Hebrews will not have to endure their punishment much longer. Their endurance has paid off. The Maccabees, however, do not intend to sit by and wait.

Personal Preparation

1. Read Daniel 5 and 1 Maccabees 1–2. Who is responsible for Israel's well-being in each case, God or the people? Both? This week, think about what is up to God and what is up to you.

2. King Belshazzar and King Antiochus IV Epiphanes didn't seem to learn anything from their predecessors about ruling justly. When have you been able to learn from the mistakes or experiences of people who came before you? Why is it so difficult to learn from history?

3. Belshazzar and Antiochus IV Epiphanes idolized power. What things or people do you idolize? To what extent do these idolatries distract you from Christian faith and life?

Understanding

Legendary baseball player Yogi Berra is perhaps better known for his manner of speaking. Expressions like "It ain't over till it's over," "That place is so crowded no one goes there anymore," "It's like *deja vu* all over again," and his response to the waiter who asked him if he wanted his pizza cut in four or eight slices ("Better cut it into four. I don't think I could eat eight.") have become legend. They are so legendary that no one, not even Yogi, is really sure he said all the things attributed to him.

One of his less well-known sayings is "History helps us to better understand the past," which is, of course, a version of the traditional "History helps us to better understand the present." Regardless of who said what, the fact is neither statement is generally true. The lessons of history are usually ignored. The fact that there is still ethnic cleansing in our time suggests we didn't learn anything from the genocide of Jews, Armenians, American Indians, and others earlier in our century. Racial tensions today mean the lessons of the civil rights struggle of the 1950s and '60s didn't last. Sadly, we haven't learned much from our history.

It's not that we're slow learners. This has been a problem through the ages, including the time in which the Book of Daniel was written. In the first four stories of Daniel, the powerful Nebuchadnezzar is changed and humbled. Daniel helps him see the supremacy of the God of Israel until Nebuchadnezzar can finally proclaim it for himself. But this lesson is soon forgotten. Like the pharaoh in Exodus who forgot about Joseph and all he had done for Egypt, Belshazzar never grasps the lessons taught to the previous ruler.

It's unclear precisely how much time elapses between Nubuchadnezzar and Belshazzar and how quickly the lessons are lost. The scripture refers to Belshazzar as Nebuchadnezzar's son, but strictly speaking Belshazzar was his grandson. When Nebuchadnezzar died in the year 562 B.C., he was succeeded by three rulers until Belshazzar's father, Nabonidus, ascended the throne. However, because Nabonidus was out of the country for much of his reign, Belshazzar ruled in his stead.

A Matter of Time

As the story opens in the year 539 B.C., the Persian emperor Cyrus is closing in on Babylon. All around are the signs that the Babylonian empire is going to fall. It's just a matter of time. How does King Belshazzar deal with the problem? Like a lot of people before and after him, he chooses to ignore his troubles altogether. Party. Party. Party. Forget about it. Ignore it. The problem will go away. Only it won't. Belshazzar, your days are numbered. Maybe ours are too.

In the United States great strides have been made with regard to civil rights, but the fact remains there is also a tremendous gulf between people of different races and ethnic groups. It's easier to ignore problems than to do the hard work of change. But it is really just a matter of time until race riots, church burnings, and million man marches get our attention and force us to change. Still the temptation is to try to solve the problem with a quick fix and forget about it.

As congregations it is easy to ignore the signs that our churches are dying. You probably know the excuses. Membership is down, but only five percent from last year. There may be no new babies, but there have been no deaths for a few months either. Things aren't so bad. And after all, we like each other. We're a friendly church—toward each other anyway. Of course we'd welcome people from the community if they wanted to attend, but somehow they don't seem to get the message that they're welcome.

As individuals we ignore problems as well. The doctor tells us to cut down on fat and it works for a week. We recycle paper, cans, and plastic when we have time. We diabetics avoid sugar until someone offers us just a sliver of pie. Our children act up in school, but that's just because they're teenagers, right? Maybe our high blood pressure would go down if we got different jobs with fewer pressures.

Belshazzar not only ignores the problem of the Persian empire, he proves he's learned nothing from history. His distinguished ancestor Nebuchadnezzar finally realized he could conquer the nation of Israel, but he could not conquer Israel's God. God Most High was more powerful than kings and empires.

This brash new ruler goes so far as to profane this God. First he drinks from the cups taken away from the temple of Jerusalem, and then he toasts other gods with them as well. Unlike his grandfather, Belshazzar assumes that just because Israel was conquered, its God was conquered as well. He learns the hard way that God's fortunes are not tied to our own. God determines who will rule; Belshazzar proves his unworthiness by drinking from the temple vessels. The great weight of God's hand is about to land upon him.

God's response to Belshazzar's profanation of the temple vessels is swift and terrible. It begins when a mysterious hand appears at a dinner party in the palace and writes a message on the wall. The New Revised Standard Version of the Bible says, "Then the king's face turned pale, and his thoughts terrified him. His limbs gave way, and his knees knocked together" (5:6). The third clause is literally "his hip joints went loose."

As was the case in earlier chapters, the king's enchanters are not able to interpret the handwriting, but the queen, who was probably Nebuchadnezzar's wife and not Belshazzar's mother, reminds him about Daniel. Belshazzar calls Daniel before him, praises him greatly, and offers great rewards if he will interpret the mysterious handwriting.

Daniel has proven he is not afraid to speak before great rulers. His life is not as important as the truth. But while he had addressed Nebuchadnezzar with respect, his attitude toward Belshazzar might be described with a little Shakespeare: "Scorn and defiance, slight regard, contempt, and anything that may not misbecome the mighty sender" (*Henry V*). Although Daniel is largely sympathetic to rulers, there are times when the regime can only be condemned. Kind of like Popeye: "I've stood all I can and I can't stands no more." Belshazzar, your days are numbered.

Conflict of Interest

Daniel refuses the gift offered by the king. He recognizes there is such a thing as "conflict of interest." The problem is this: if you receive money from someone you're supposed to critique, can you be objective? I review plays for a newspaper, and I struggle with the issue of whether I should accept free tickets from the theaters where I review plays. If I accept a free ticket, will I feel I should give every show a good review? I also write feature articles for a newspaper. When I was hired by a local hospital to write their press releases, I called my editor at the newspaper and told him I would no longer write articles about the hospital's activities for him. I didn't think it was ethical to accept money from the hospital to promote the hospital and at the same time accept money from the newspaper to possibly critique the hospital. There is a conflict of interest between writing *for* an institution and writing *about* it.

Pastors struggle with conflict of interest when it comes to paid ministry. They have to decide how prophetic they can be from the pulpit with the people who dole out the paychecks. If, on the other hand, a pastor is paid by the denomination and not the congregation, how is he or she held accountable?

Belshazzar seems to feel he can buy his salvation by paying Daniel. He wants to hear what he pays for. It reminds me of a joke my Dad tells about a man who insists to St. Peter that he has a right to get into heaven because he put a buck in the offering plate once upon a time. After conferring with a higher authority by phone, St. Peter relays the message that his Boss says the man can keep his dollar and go to hell.

Daniel refuses to be used by this politician. Belshazzar cannot buy deliverance by buying Daniel. Daniel values the truth more than he values the regard of a corrupt ruler. It's worth noting, however, that Daniel does accept the reward at the end of the story, but only because the king insists. Daniel had already taken his stand and made it clear that his message would be delivered without thought of reward.

Half Dollar, Half Dollar, Penny, Two Bits

Back to the story. Daniel reminds Belshazzar of his ancestry's experience with God Most High, and he mocks Belshazzar's idols, pointing out that they will not help him. The effect of this whole sequence is to increase the suspense. We still don't know what the words on the wall mean, but by now we suspect it can't be good. Finally Daniel interprets the message on the wall.

Originally, written Hebrew employed only consonants. The word *Hebrew*, for instance, would be spelled *hbrw*. Marks were added later to indicate vowels, but only after Hebrew ceased to be a living language. It was possible in most cases to tell what the word was from the consonants only. But there were occasions when two words used the same consonants. If the same system were used in English, the letters *crt*, for instance, could signify a cart, a court, or a crate. Without vowels, it's difficult to know the precise word.

The words *Mene, Mene, Tekel,* and *Parsin* in Hebrew could be, on the one hand, the consonants for a set of measures or coins. On the other hand, they form a message that can be read. Taken together they have an interesting double meaning. On the face of things, Paul Lederach suggests the words can be translated into the modern terms "Half dollar, half dollar, cent, two bits." Sticking to the theme of weights and measures, Daniel gives them deeper meaning for Belshazzar. *Mene,* your days have been measured. *Tekel,* you have been weighed and found wanting. *Parsin,* your kingdom will be divided between the Medes and Persians.

As mentioned earlier, most biblical prophecies of doom include an out, or an "if." If you continue to do such and such, bad things will happen, but if you repent, you can avoid doom. Nebuchadnezzar would have repented if he had received such a message. At least for a while. But there is no out offered to Belshazzar, perhaps because God knows he will not repent. Nor does Belshazzar resist his fate. Instead, after giving Daniel the great reward, Belshazzar seems to be resigned to his fate, which follows shortly. He is doomed. Soon he is dead.

Is this resignation realistic? I think so. Like the man in Christopher Marlowe's *Dr. Faustus* who sells his soul to the devil, bewails his fate, and cries aloud in torment, some people do everything but ask for forgiveness. But I have seen others who, with glassy stare, ignore the way to wholeness and accept their doom with apathy, because they will not give up their idol, whether it be a television set, a car, or a shaker of salt.

Historical records show that the Persian conquest was largely bloodless. Many Babylonians looked to the Persians not as conquerors, but as liberators. The histories do not agree on the exact method that was used to capture the city, and the scripture is not interested in giving any details, but all sources agree it happened quickly.

Daniel's message is clear for all systems that wantonly violate the laws of God. You have been weighed in the balance and have been found wanting. Your days are numbered. Tyrants perish. This is encouraging news to those who suffer under tyrants, whose rule seems eternal. Those who believe they are above the law will be judged.

Sometimes we take too great a comfort in this passage, assuming its message is for tyrants around the globe and not for ourselves. But Belshazzar's sin is the sin of many world leaders, some who are outright sinister. In his commentary on Daniel, Daniel L. Christopher-Smith writes about the Belshazzars of the western world who also profaned holy sites and eradicated cultures. He notes, for instance, how "Pacific native peoples bitterly recall the desecration of holy sites by Captain Cook, and today's Cheyenne recount another 'Belshazzar's Feast'—the parade of bloody body parts of slain Cheyenne through downtown Denver following the 1864 Sand Creek Massacre. . . . Defeat and destruction are never enough for the powerful; they must also glorify themselves with acts of unspeakable humiliation of the defeated."

But there are also more subtle acts against other cultures. For many years, American road builders, miners, developers, and museum curators have carelessly destroyed burial grounds, desecrated holy sites, and carted off the treasures of American Indian groups in the name of progress and learning. And we the public have used the roads and the ore and enjoyed the museums without ever thinking that we were profaning a holy site or humiliating a people. A 1990 Native American Graves Protection and Repatriation Act seeks to end such humiliation.

Daniel outlived the Babylonian occupation. That is triumph enough right there. We can only assume that God is in charge of history.

The Hammer

First Maccabees also demonstrates that God is at work in history, but not through direct intervention as in Daniel. In 1 Maccabees, God works through the people of faith. The book was likely written between 135 and 100 B.C., but talks about the generation before, 175–143 B.C. It deals with the Jewish rebellion against the oppressive ruler Antiochus IV Epiphanes, who reigned when the Book of Daniel was likely written down.

While describing the facts with great accuracy, the intent of 1 Maccabees is to highlight the family that eventually developed into the Hasmonean Dynasty. The book also urges God's people to rise up and defend themselves and criticizes those who sit passively by, waiting for God to do something. It is a tough question for us. When is it faithful to wait, and when is it faithful to act?

The passage from 1 Maccabees records the events that led to the great revolt, which is celebrated in the feast of Chanukah. This is a remarkably heroic story in light of the fact that Antiochus IV Epiphanes persecuted the Jews horribly and profaned the temple. He did all this to destroy Hebrew culture and force Judah to live as Gentiles. Where Greek ways did not conflict with their faith, Jews had always before adopted them freely, but this ruler attempted to force them on the people, causing Jews to cross the line of propriety. If they complied with his mandates, they could no longer remain faithful to Yahweh.

Under the leadership of Judas Maccabeus (the Hammer) and his sons after him, some Jews stood up to the foreign king and eventually reclaimed the temple. They reinstituted worship as required by scripture and finally, after some years, drove foreigners from the land and instituted an independent nation. Thanks to the heroism of the Maccabees, the foreign yoke was thrown off and freedom restored to the people.

In 1 Maccabees, its heroes are compared to the heroes of the Old Testament, even referring to the stories of the three young men in the fiery furnace and Daniel in the lion's den (1 Macc. 2:59-60). But the view of the author is that those who practice nonviolent resistance are foolish and unsuccessful. Those who believe their faith forbids them to fight or disobey sabbath laws deserve their fate. (See 1 Maccabees 1:53-64; 2:29-38.) Martyrdom and resurrection are not factors in this book, in contrast to 2 Maccabees, which praises faithfulness and credits the victory to the prayers of the faithful and the sacrifice of the martyrs.

For all their heroism and decisiveness, the victory of the Maccabees is only temporary. Strife between the rival families leads to later enslavement. The Maccabees have triumphed. For a time. Make no mistake. First Maccabees is fascinating reading, illustrating how a people resists religious oppression. When I read this book I root for the Maccabees. I wouldn't be surprised if you're not tempted to read the whole book once you've begun it. It's one of my favorite readings. But it has its limitations.

When all is said and done, 1 Maccabees describes what happened. The Book of Daniel tells us what was really going on. Tyrants will perish. God is in charge. Daniel also looks ahead to an eternal kingdom that cannot be overthrown and whose ruler is divine and eternal. That's the subject of the seventh chapter and beyond. Hold on!

Discussion and Action

1. As a group, name some of the hot religious and political issues of the day. Would you say you have a tendency to take too much responsibility for the world's problems, or not enough? How can you personally help resolve some of these issues, even international conflict? What should be left up to God? Pick one of these issues and take an action, such as writing letters to government leaders, contributing money to a hunger organization, offering to spend time working in a food pantry, doing odd jobs, cleaning up the environment, or staffing a homeless shelter.

2. Think about your family history for a few minutes. If you can, tell about mistakes you think your grandparents or parents made in their lives. Have you learned from their mistakes? How? Why is it so difficult to learn from others' mistakes? What do you hope the next generation will learn from you?

3. King Belshazzar ignored his problems until it was too late. How do you handle problems? Give each other tips on taking care of problems. If members of the group need a friend to help make decisions and face problems, divide into pairs to encourage each other in the future as you make decisions.

4. Daniel won't offer advice for money. If he is paid, he feels he must tell the king what he wants to hear. Tell the group about a time you faced a conflict of interest as a student, a parent, a business person, a church member, or in some other capacity.

5. In the church, what conflict does a pastor face as he or she preaches for a salary? What should the congregation expect for the salary they pay? How willing are you to listen to criticism from the pulpit?

6. If we fail to keep our part of our covenant with God, we can, like Nebuchadnezzar, repent. How do you repent? Is it enough to say you're sorry? What else can you do?

7. Which seems like the better way to combat tyranny, Daniel's way or Judas Maccabeus's way? Why? Who are the modern Daniels and the modern Maccabeuses?

6

The Lion's Den
Daniel 6; Bel and the Dragon; Susanna

Daniel triumphs while those who plotted against him suffer the fate they intended for the innocent. The same is true for Susanna and for Bel and the Dragon. God will deliver the faithful.

Personal Preparation

1. Read Daniel 6, Bel and the Dragon, and Susanna. How do the two apocryphal stories about Daniel resemble the Book of Daniel? How do they differ?
2. Recall some of the folktales or fairy tales you learned as a child. What kernel of truth is there in each one? Be prepared to tell your favorite story to the group.
3. When has the law worked against you even though you were right? How did the situation end? When have you, like Daniel, been delivered from an injustice?

Understanding

Elisha Hunt Rhodes, made famous by Ken Burns's television series on the Civil War, joined the ranks of the Union army at the outset of the war and, by coincidence, was present at virtually every significant battle of the conflict. Through it all he kept a diary that now tells us a great deal about the daily life of soldiers in his era.

The diary also tells that Rhodes, no matter how trying the circumstances, made an effort to worship every Sunday. Whether in the field, in camp, in friendly villages, or in occupied Confederate territory, Rhodes would worship. And he often made a note or two about the subject and quality of the sermon.

Toward the end of the war, Rhodes worshiped in Confederate churches where he endured many sermons against the Union and his uniform. As part of the conquering army, of course, Rhodes expected Christians in the Confederacy to be hostile. And while he bore considerable discomfort, the danger was probably no greater than what he had faced many times during the war.

Daniel is in a far more difficult position. He's on the losing side. As a Hebrew in Babylon, he is virtually the slave of the ruler. In chapter 6, a new ruler has taken power. Daniel no longer serves Nebuchadnezzar, but Darius, king of the Medes. (Darius is a fictional character. Cyrus the Persian follows Nebuchadnezzar in history.) Though Darius favors Daniel, Daniel still serves as a slave without rights.

The Persians overtake the Babylonian empire, and, initially at least, they grant a high degree of religious and social freedom to the conquered nations living there. They demand tribute to support the empire, but at the same time they allow groups such as the Jews to return to their homelands and to worship as they see fit. This is in contrast to the policies of earlier rulers who tried to stamp out ethnic identities.

But despite the relative tolerance and openness, Daniel experiences religious persecution at the hands of his captors. His treatment does not come at the will of the king, but as the result of office politics. Having recognized Daniel's worth as a servant, the king has elevated him to a high position, and loyal courtiers, because of professional jealousy, try to bring him down.

The Crime of Being Different

The year 1492 is a turning point in history, though not for the reason usually given. In that year the Spaniards drove the Moors out of their country and expelled the Jews. Islamic and Jewish culture had greatly enriched Spain in the sciences, arts, and literature, and to no small degree contributed to the nation's strength and prestige. With the loss of ethnic and religious diversity, the nation was irretrievably weakened and did not recover for centuries.

The Persians also benefited from the know-how of the people they conquered, but, like Spain, the ruling elite didn't want to share authority or prosperity with aliens like Daniel. Getting rid of Daniel on religious grounds is only a cover for simple office politics. This is the case in many religious wars today. If the truth be known, there is far less concern for religious piety than there is for seizing control of power, often in God's name. And as in Spain, the selfish grab for power by one group impoverishes a whole nation, robbing it of skillful leaders and thinkers.

Daniel is a victim of his own success, having achieved his position because of his skill, and he suffers under good old-fashioned office politics. His colleagues, like ours, are simply jealous of another's success or view others as roadblocks in the path to their own success. To these individuals there can't be winners without losers. This may be true in some board games, but in the modern world, things are better when we increase the number of winners. Take world economics for example. Another country's economic misfortune, far from signaling a victory for our country, can harm us by reducing the markets for our goods.

Office politics is especially hard to fight, because so much depends on outward smiling faces and inward desires to backstab. The courtiers know that Daniel is Darius's pet. They can't risk being openly hostile without falling out of favor with the king. They create a way for Daniel to fail on his own. They ask everyone in the kingdom to pray to the king for thirty days. If they cannot, they will be executed. They depend on Daniel's piety to destroy him, and it does at the outset. In this story, Daniel maintains his integrity by continuing to live life as always, in an atmosphere of prayer to God. For this they give him the death penalty—the lion's den.

Churches are hardly exempt from this sort of maneuvering. Recently, at a church in my area, a pastor suddenly resigned one Sunday. Half the church had no idea there was any problem or any politicking going on. But from the members gathered in small groups in the parking lot after church, furtively looking over their shoulders, leaning in toward one another, speaking in hushed tones, it was clear that some of them had arranged for the quick departure and that their reasons were dishonest.

Jealousy

While Darius's minions are the villains in the story, it's not hard to imagine that Daniel truly irritated them with his great piety. From the beginning Daniel seems too good to be true. And while we'd all like to identify with Daniel, we can more likely sympathize with his colleagues, because we've all worked with someone who was "holier than thou," a "goody-two-shoes," who drove us crazy. In such a situation, it's easy to allow ourselves to be jealous of a very good person, looking for his or her little imperfections and magnifying them as large as possible. I have to wonder if I would really like Daniel if I knew him and worked with him.

Daniel even prays in full view of the others, making us wonder if he is flaunting his piety. This passage reminds me that Jesus counseled his disciples to pray in secret, so only the Father in heaven would know. Was Daniel acting contrary to this? Perhaps. But Jesus was speaking to those who hoped to gain the better opinion of others because of their public piety. Daniel was putting his life in danger. Bible scholar John Goldingay says, "When prayer is fashionable it is time to pray in secret (Matt 6:5-6), but when prayer is under pressure, to pray in secret is to give the appearance of fearing the king more than God." Daniel prayed under pressure!

The early Christians faced the same choice—obey God or earthly rulers. In some cases those who obeyed God and suffered were delivered, as when Peter was released from prison in Acts 12. But others who obeyed were executed, as were Stephen and James the brother of the Lord. It's not that God failed them. Their deaths were their victories, for their martyrdom proved the ultimate validation of their faith.

That kind of witness continued past the time of the apostles. On a February day in the year 156, Polycarp, the overseer of the church in Smyrna, was arrested on the charge of practicing the Christian faith. In his youth he had known the Apostle John and others who knew the Lord in the flesh.

> [At his trial] he was brought forward to the Proconsul, who asked him if he were Polycarp. When he said he was one and the same, he tried to dissuade him, saying, "Remember your age. . . . Swear allegiance (to Caesar) and I'll release you." Polycarp answered, "I have been his slave eighty-six years and he has never treated me unjustly. How is it possible I should blaspheme my king who saved me?" (*Martyrdom of Polycarp* 9:2,3)

Polycarp was burned at the stake and did not die until he was pierced through the heart with a dagger.

In Daniel's time, fire was sacred in the Persians' Zoroastrian faith and was not used as capital punishment. Instead, Daniel is thrown to the lions for his obedience to his God. But note that, like Pilate, King Darius feels trapped by the law he allowed himself to be talked into.

The fact is that certain laws are unjust and must be disobeyed. Defying unjust laws (civil disobedience) is an honored tradition from Daniel to Socrates to Jesus to the martyrs to the present, though each had to go through a personal fire and not around it. They may have been vindicated ultimately, but initially they suffered. According to biographer Daniel Smith-Christopher, Mahatma Gandhi said he had "found much consolation in reading the book of the prophet Daniel in the Bible." Gandhi saw Daniel as "one of the greatest passive resisters that ever lived" and took great solace in the book during his work in South Africa and India.

The powerful often view the faithful, the meek, the nonviolent as dangerous, and they are. Nonviolence subverts the powerful and disarms the hateful. Not wanting to lose their position, the powerful degrade the meek and the nonviolent. For instance, Daniel's co-workers make him out to be disloyal and a danger to the king.

Not long ago a young woman named Jennifer Casolo went to El Salvador to work with an ecumenical program called Christian Education Seminars. It was her job to educate North Americans about injustice in El Salvador during its long war. Salvadoran authorities considered her dangerous and powerful because she told people the truth about government injustices. They knew that those who come in the name of Christ are so powerful they can topple regimes without firing a shot.

To stop Jennifer, the Salvadoran government arrested her on trumped up charges of stockpiling weapons and held her for several weeks in 1989. Like Daniel, she did not lie to protect herself. She went to prison, willing to accept the consequences of telling the truth. And like Daniel, she was delivered. All during her captivity she preached the gospel of love to her captors and proved what has been true for two thousand years—persecution doesn't work.

Meanwhile in Persia

The king is horrified that he must condemn a trusted counselor to death for the crime of praying three times a day, but he consigns Daniel to his fate while expressing the hope that Daniel's God will deliver him. After a sleepless night, Darius unseals the pit and discovers Daniel is alive. Until this point Daniel has said nothing, but when he speaks, he proclaims God's glory and great deeds.

When everything is said and done, this story isn't about Daniel's great faithfulness, or lions, or evil empires. It's the story of God's power, which Daniel keeps trying to proclaim. God is the primary actor in the drama, interpreting dreams and delivering people from fiery furnaces and lion dens. Daniel's action is to be an instrument for God, to respond when God calls. We have the same task. We respond to God. We love because God first loves us.

The Apocrypha

Perhaps the most important thing about the story is that Darius, a pagan king, proclaims Daniel's God as "the living God" (6:26). The message of the nations from the Aramaic portion of Daniel is that, in contrast to gods of stone and gold, God is active in history, not remote. He is a living God who hears and delivers when he chooses.

The two sets of stories from the Apocrypha, Bel and the Dragon and Susanna, also proclaim the living God. They appear as chapters 13 and 14 of Daniel in Catholic versions of the Bible. Their language and tone make it clear that they were originally included in the collection we know as Daniel, but their preservation is proof enough that there were probably many stories circulating about this historical figure. The Gospel of John says that if all the stories about Jesus were collected in one place, the world itself could probably not hold them all. In the case of Daniel, it's possible that the stories about Daniel, if collected, would probably fill at least a few shelves.

Like the stories in chapters 3 and 6, the two stories in Bel and the Dragon might be called *confrontation stories*, emphasizing the conflict that exists between religion and government. Both also demonstrate the folly of idol worship.

In the first story, Cyrus claims that the great statue of Bel is a living god because it eats the food which is offered to it. Daniel offers to prove otherwise. Ahead of his time in forensics, Daniel sprinkles ashes on the floor, knowing the temple functionaries who have created the charade that the idol is alive will leave their footprints when they enter the sealed chamber through trapdoors to eat the food left for the statue.

There are plenty of stories from ancient history in which food was offered ceremoniously to an idol and then split among the temple functionaries for meals. In this story, however, the priests of Bel manipulate a religious image for their own benefit, pretending the idol actually ate the food. As transparent as this might seem, we also have our share of religious manipulators today. They hide behind the cross, using it for their financial gain, quoting scripture as they ask for more and more and more money to support their ministries and sometimes their appetites.

In the second part of the chapter, Cyrus wants Daniel to admit that at least the great serpent they worship is a living god. Daniel also disproves this by feeding the beast "pitchburgers," killing it with indigestion (Bel and Dragon 27). The people are enraged and demand Daniel's execution. Cyrus caves in. Once again Daniel is placed in a den of lions, this time for six days. At the end of that time, an angel carries the prophet Habakkuk (who historically lived fifty years before that time) by a hank of his hair to the lion's den to offer a bowl of soup to Daniel before whisking him back home. Daniel's God is revealed again to be the only true, living God.

Susanna is the story of Daniel, boy detective. It seems to take place at the beginning of the Babylonian captivity, and in some manuscripts it appears as the first chapter of Daniel. In the story, two elders lust after the virtuous Susanna, but when they finally trap her, she refuses to give in to their sexual demands. Whether or not she succumbs, the elders vow they will tell the people she is an adulteress and have her stoned to death to protect their own reputations. Susanna loses either way. When the case is brought before the people, they are swayed by the appearance of things and the honor of the elders. To no one's surprise, the scoundrels win.

As Susanna is being marched away to be stoned, the Spirit of God directs Daniel to intervene. He uses the same technique employed by the professor who faced two students who claimed they were late for a final exam because of a flat tire. The professor separated the two students and gave them a two-question exam. The first question, worth five points, was simply, What's two plus two? The second question, worth ninety-five points, was, Which tire was flat?

Daniel asks the two elders under which tree they supposedly discovered Susanna committing adultery. They each give a different answer, proving they witnessed no such thing. Susanna is vindicated and the devious elders are condemned to the same fate intended for her. The moral of this story and the stories of Daniel in the lion's den is that God delivers the faithful. And often the wicked suffer in the same way as those they have persecuted.

A modern day innocent who was delivered in a similar way is King Christian of Denmark during World War II. The Nazis overran Denmark and declared that all Jews be marked with the yellow Star of David, a mark of condemnation in the Nazi period. Unwilling to turn over thousands of innocent people to murderous Nazis, Christian appeared at the appointed day and time wearing a yellow Star of David himself, as were all the citizens of Denmark. Suddenly the Nazis could not tell who was Jewish and who was not. By his faith and his cleverness, Christian and the Jews were delivered, and the persecutors were completely confounded.

Once Upon a Time

Virtually every household in the United States has a television. In addition to talk shows, sports, and news, people are hooked on drama. Though not technically true, television dramas about families, hospitals, police, and society have a tremendous impact on people, inspiring them to take up action for a cause, shaping what they think about social issues, and resonating deeply with personal experiences. In this sense, television drama is true. And in this sense, stories of the Apocrypha are also true. The stories are true even if they are not factual or historical. Anyone who has experienced God's love and grace in tough times knows at least this one truth—that God delivers the faithful.

The Book of Daniel is probably true in the same way. The larger lessons we learn from it are far more important than any consideration of their historical value. The Good Samaritan and the Prodigal Son, both fictional characters in parables told by Jesus, are far more real to us and have a greater effect on our lives than such historical people as Presidents Millard Fillmore and William Henry Harrison!

Many stories of the Bible are proverbs, stories or parables, stories for illustration, and the collected and tested wisdom of the community of faith. While Daniel was likely a real person, these stories about him are God-revealed folklore used to teach people about a life of faith.

Our Jewish ancestors did not include Daniel with the other prophets. Instead, they put this book in the section of the Old Testament known as the Writings, because they realized it was different from Isaiah, Jeremiah, and Ezekiel. It's not in the Prophets, but it's in the Bible and its teachings are true.

Believers have the duty to study the wise stories of faith to discover what is useful and true and what God is trying to say through them. That's what we do when we study the Bible, but it's possible to get the story wrong, to fail to see the truth God intended in it. Folksinger Carrie Newcome tells how once as a very young girl she asked her mother why she always cut off the end of the Easter ham and put it in a separate glass pan. The mother did it because her mother did it, and her mother did it because the great grandmother did it. In her late nineties, the great grandmother revealed the reason she cut off the end of the ham and cooked it separately. It was because her oven wasn't large enough for the whole ham. Each generation has to read the stories and find the truth of God for itself.

The stories of Daniel, grounded in some history and some truth-telling, encourage us to remain faithful in the face of opposition, to be God's people in difficult circumstances, and to trust in God's vindication, knowing that in life and even in death—sometimes especially in death—we are delivered.

Discussion and Action

1. Tell your favorite folktale from your childhood. What important truths did you learn from these stories?

2. Is it possible to be faithful as Daniel was faithful? Why or why not? Who have you known personally who was saintly? What attracts you or puts you off about this person?

3. In pairs, talk about how you would like to be more faithful at church, in your family, at work, and in your community. In the larger group, exchange ideas for ways to be more disciplined about faith. What has worked for you that will help others?

4. Switch from identifying with Daniel or Susanna and identify for a minute with King Darius. Tell about a time you were silent like Darius when you should have spoken up about an injustice against someone else. What consequences have you lived with since then?

5. Also identify with Darius's servants. What is the greatest jealousy you have ever felt? What did you do about it? How do you keep jealousy in check in your life?

6. How has God delivered you or someone you know? If God delivers the faithful, why do good people still suffer? Be instruments of God's deliverance. Learn about someone in your group or congregation who needs visits, help with meals, odd jobs, or transportation, and offer to help out next week.

God of All History—
The Ancient of Days
Daniel 7; the Letter of Jeremiah

God is not just the Lord of the Afterlife. God is Lord of History—past and present. Daniel knows that God's kingdom will come even as God's people are abused and suffering.

Personal Preparation

1. Read Daniel 7 and the Letter to Jeremiah in the Apocrypha. Recall the definition of apocalyptic literature from chapter 1, which says that apocalyptic stories are meant to encourage people living in hard times by assuring them that God is in control of history, that evil will ultimately be defeated, and that heaven and earth are related. What happens in one happens in the other. How is Daniel 7 an apocalyptic story?
2. Apocalyptic stories often come from dreams and visions. Call to mind an especially vivid dream or prophetic vision you have had. How does it fit the definition of an apocalyptic dream?
3. What credence do you give dreams and visions? Why is it difficult to make dreams a reality?

Understanding

Some people are afraid of snakes or rats. I'm not too hot on spiders, so when I had a dream about an enormous spider years ago, it was a virtual nightmare. In the dream I was peeling a banana, only to find a big, yellow, hairy spider under the peel and not a banana at all.

Real horror crept over me. Nightmare time. Except this dream was different. I grew annoyed, and while I was sleeping I remember saying to myself, I don't have dreams like this anymore. I don't think I've had a nightmare since. I've had sad dreams and frustrating dreams, but not a full-blown nightmare. Praise be to God. Daniel did not seem to have that kind of luck. When your dreams come from God, you can't get yourself out of it. One thing is certain. When the visions start, they can't be stopped by the receiver. You can wake from a dream if it's frightening. If the show is upsetting, you can switch the channel. You can even turn off the TV or walk out of the movie theater. But a vision is for real.

Chapter 7 begins a new section of the Book of Daniel. There is a dramatic shift from storytelling to records of dreams and visions, something like Zechariah or Ezekiel, or Revelation. Did Daniel rise and look out his window at night and see the visions against the starry sky? Were they projected on a wall? or on the inside of his eyelids? Was it terrifying?

I'm sure an encounter with godliness would frighten me terribly, mostly because it's not always easy to understand what God reveals. When you've looked into eternity, you know that the message doesn't always translate well into human terms. Look at Moses and company who saw the God of Israel. "Under his feet there was something like a pavement of sapphire stone, like the very heaven for clearness" (Exod. 24:10). But it is only *like* sapphires, it is not sapphire. And in Revelation "there is something like a sea of glass, like crystal" (Rev. 4:6), but it is neither glass or crystal. It is only like them. How can we ever explain what we've experienced?

Although this section of Daniel changes dramatically in style from the first half of the book, the message is the same. God is the Lord of history. All oppressed and suffering people should hold on a little longer.

Who's Who? What's What?

Among the elements in Daniel's dream is the use of animals to represent other nations. The beasts in this vision are unclean animals according to Jewish law. They represent the gentile people at their worst. The first, the lion with majestic wings, is lordlike and swift to kill in judgment. It represents the Babylonians. The second beast is the bear, representing the Medes. This is a strange bear. It is told to "arise, devour many bodies!" (7:5). Empires lie broken at its feet.

After the bear, a leopardlike being also arises. This winged creature represents the Persians. They created their empire on a foundation made from the fallen empires of Ur, Elba, Sumer, and Babylon.

The fourth beast seen in the night visions is terrible and dreadful and exceedingly strong. Great iron teeth, ten horns, stamping feet. It may have been a dragon. Representing at first the glorious conqueror Alexander the Great, the beast soon becomes Antiochus. This was the crisis facing the writer and many of the first readers of Daniel.

Swiftly they rise and swiftly they fall, at least in retrospect. As a child I remember the fleeting Cuban Missile Crisis when the world came close to nuclear war. I assumed then that nuclear standoffs would be a fact of life for my children and grandchildren. But this crisis passed. After all is said and done, it's best not to associate the animals with specific nations, because they could refer to hundreds of regimes, including the U.S. and the Soviet Union, that have come and gone in the twinkling of an eye as in these visions.

Once I gathered with other pastors in a cabin high in the California mountains. The beauty of nature surrounded us, but we were still aware of the troubles in the world. Then one of the pastors, Desmond Bittinger, told us about the time he spoke to some Chinese who had endured and survived the Cultural Revolution. "This communism stuff will never last," they told him. "Four hundred years at most." The Chinese, Bittinger said, took the long view, the view espoused by Daniel.

Still, it's easier to say in retrospect that empires have passed away than it is to trust that evil empires of our day will dwindle and fade. Though Daniel was written down when Israel was suffering under Antiochus IV Epiphanes in the second century B.C., the story is told as if it happened during the first year of Babylon's last king, the ill-fated Belshazzar we met in chapter 5. The events, however, speak specifically to the trials of God's people during the Maccabean crisis hundreds of years later.

Who Shall Stand?

Who shall stand against the beast when God's people are scattered like sheep? None other than the Perfect Shepherd who is a sheep like they and who will sacrifice himself for them. Who indeed! Part of the message of Daniel's vision is that you ain't seen nothing yet. There is one coming who is far more powerful than any worldly king. It is the Lamb who in Revelation appears with the mark of sacrifice but who is the champion over the beast.

But in this vision, we see the Lamb as he really is—the Ancient of Days. His throne is fiery flames and there are wheels of burning fires. He is attended by uncounted heavenly beings. Maybe the beasts aren't so powerful after all. Even though the beast is filling the air with "the noise of the arrogant words" (7:11), it is destroyed effortlessly.

You wanted a terrible God? You've got one. The pure images of heaven seem too terrifying, impossible to endure. So this God is filtered for his followers through "one like a human being, coming with the clouds of heaven" (7:13). To this one is given power and dominion. Many Christians identify this "one like a human being" (called "son of man" in some translations) to be Jesus. The New Testament uses language in its own apocalyptic sections that identify Jesus with this person of power.

"As for me, Daniel, my spirit was troubled within me, and the visions of my head terrified me" (7:15). He still wants to know about the fourth beast, because that is the trial that is being endured by God's people. And so assurance is given again in a great song of triumph that the kingdom established by God is an eternal one and that the worldly kingdoms endure only for a while.

We're going to win. That's the central message of the scripture. No matter how horrible the monster, we're going to win. Each day there are new headlines. Old monsters are relegated to the back pages and a new enemy emerges. Even kingdoms that should seemingly last forever fade away in the face of our God.

Christians daringly proclaimed that Jesus, so brutally and shamefully executed, had in fact risen from the dead and would return in glory. For them Antiochus was a dead memory. Now it was the brutal Nero who concerned them, and it was the words of Daniel that provided them with comfort, encouragement, and reassurance that even Nero would pass away.

Which is one of the reasons it isn't so important to tie each beast to a particular kingdom. Some people who do this end up associating the beasts with the tyrants of our time. They are right and wrong when they do this. They are wrong to use their schemes to calendarize God's plan, pushing and shoving current rulers into visionary clothes, which don't fit that well, so they can state with confidence that the end time is now. But they are right in that the vision describes the plight of God's people under tyrants throughout time like Antiochus, Nero, Domitian, and Hitler. The Anabaptists who were brutally persecuted by state churches would have been right in associating the beasts with those who mocked Christ by killing in his name. And we are correct in making parallels between the beasts and our own time as long as we realize our children and our children's children will also be justified in doing so.

We Win!

Daniel 7 is typical apocalyptic writing. It uses a vision to preach that God's kingdom will come and evil will be dethroned at the end of time.

Some ask, Why speak in apocalyptic terms? Couldn't something be said more clearly about God's work in the world without mysterious visions? Just as some things are better said through song and poetry and others through essays and still others through humor, there are advantages to this graphic form of expression. Apocalyptic stories, like television programs, are very visual and very memorable. Many of us can remember specific episodes of our favorite situation comedies and even more readily the theme songs and advertising jingles we learned from television as children. Apocalyptic stories have the same effect on us, because the dramatic stories are easy to remember. But they have their limitations as well. Some of the fine points can be lost. We remember the events of the story, but we can't remember exactly what they mean.

I have read that the text of a half-hour news broadcast will barely fill a column of text in *The New York Times*. But sometimes there is need for more than just data; visual images have as much impact as the spoken message. And impact is the primary virtue of television—and apocalyptic literature. In apocalyptic stories, the things that were theoretical become personal.

Daniel's dream makes visible what is normally invisible—God's action in the world. Sure, you say. It's visible now, and it's extraordinarily clear to Daniel, but it's still mystifying to me. Maybe you'll be comforted by the fact that Daniel's dreams became part of scripture because they are meant to be our experiences as well. They are there so that we can wrestle with their meaning just as Daniel did.

Some people prefer to believe only in the things they see. They worship stuff, their possessions, their television, their money, their power. Others know that the unseen world is more powerful. When I first arrived at the congregation I serve now, I made it a point to visit every single family. In order to learn something about their lives, I asked them all, "Where were you during the Palm Sunday tornado?" A tremendous double funnel hit the area in 1965, and several church members lost their homes. Some huddled together in the church basement because they had come for Sunday evening services. Others were at home. Each had an exciting story to tell. The wind is something powerful and unseen. What we see when we view a tornado funnel is the dust and debris swirling round and round.

The action of God's spirit is even more powerful and less visible than wind. Its action uproots more lives than any tornado. Some refuse to acknowledge its effect on their lives; others beg for it, such as John Donne, who in a sonnet prayed, "Batter my heart, three-personed God."

In our time we have been confronted by dreams and visions of different sorts. Dr. Martin Luther King, Jr., had a dream, and his dream still inspires us. Jim Jones and the doomed inhabitants of Jonestown, as well as David Koresh and the Branch Davidians, claimed their visions came from God as well, but their way led to death for themselves and their followers. So how do we tell which dreams come from God?

There is no easy answer or consistent litmus test, but I suspect that, at the very least, dreams need to be tested by the community of faith. Dr. King's dream came from his background as a servant to others and his connection to both his ethnic and religious community. Its aim was not to elevate one person but a people. The dreams of megalomaniacs are to glorify themselves and rule, not serve, others.

Another test of dreams is to see if they compare to the message of dreams already in scripture. Of course, everyone seems to be able to quote scripture to defend any cause. But if our dreams and visions are truly God's, they will be born out in the biblical story. We need to test our lives, not the scriptures, to see how well they conform to what God wants us to do, not what we want the scriptures to do.

Idols and Other Imaginings

The visible and the invisible are also the subject of the apocryphal Letter of Jeremiah, which mocks believers who turn to idols. It reminds us that just because we can see something does not mean it is powerful. All idols are ridiculous when held up to the light of day.

The Letter of Jeremiah contains its own evidence that it was not written by the prophet Jeremiah. It was composed far later. This work was written in imitation of the letter to the exiles in Jeremiah 29, but the writer is really expanding on Jeremiah 10:11, the only verse in the book written in Aramaic, the common language of a later era: "Thus shall you say to them: The gods who did not make the heavens and the earth shall perish from the earth and from under the heavens."

Just as the kings of the world are a passing fancy, as pronounced in Daniel 7, so too the Letter of Jeremiah makes it clear that the gods of this world are nothing but mist. "Like a scarecrow in a cucumber bed, which guards nothing, so are their gods of wood, overlaid with gold and silver" (Letter of Jeremiah 6:70).

Ours is a culture that prizes the things that can be touched and seen with the naked eye. We do not prize visionaries and dreamers, not at least until many years later when their dreams have come true and their visions have taken on a concrete reality. Yet scripture says, "Now faith is the assurance of things hoped for, the conviction of things not seen"

(Heb. 11:1). Our hope lies in what is unseen. Think about getting in on the ground floor of someone's dream. Maybe even your own.

Discussion and Action

1. Share notes about vivid dreams that seemed shattering at the time. What impact did these dreams have when you awoke from them? What impact do they have now, looking back on them? Try drawing an image from your dreams that is difficult to explain. Share your drawings with the group.

2. Name passages of a book, a poem, or a movie that have affected you deeply, but which seem to have made no impact on others. When our young people have visions and our older members dream dreams, do we allow them to share them, or do we disregard their ideas?

3. What is God's dream for the world? How do you know this is God's dream? Share with each other any methods for testing the validity of your dreams and visions or knowing what God's dreams are for us.

4. What do you like about apocalyptic writing in the Bible, particularly in Daniel? What mystifies you? What do you dislike about it? What frustrates you?

5. Dream dreams and see visions together. What visions do you have for the covenant group, your congregation, or yourselves as disciples of Christ? What can you do to make these dreams become reality?

6. When should we expect the kingdom to come? How has it come already? If the apocalypse came tomorrow, who would be saved from suffering?

7. Name unseen things you believe in. Also name the visible things you "believe in" or idolize. How are modern idols the same as or different from ancient idols? Make your idols come alive. Gather up things cluttering your house and sell them at a garage sale or rummage sale to raise money for a charity. Or to symbolize your ability to let go of idols, simply collect a little money to give to a charity.

8

The Fall of Babylon
Daniel 8; Revelation 18

*In a vision two beasts have a terrific fight. They represent
the nations, whom we expect to act this way. Their struggle
for power makes many people suffer, but Daniel knows that
their rule is limited by God. Soon the unholy system will be
swept away. In the meantime, life has to go on.*

Personal Preparation

1. Read Daniel 8 twice. At first, read it as a person of God who
   will be vindicated when God wins the battle with the forces of
   evil in the world. Read it again as if you were part of the forces
   of evil. This week, contemplate which side you are on.
2. Think about the battles in life you should fight. Which battles
   should you leave to God? How can you work with God for the
   right things?
3. When Daniel receives a vision, he doesn't understand it. What
   don't you understand about faith? Does it bother you that you
   don't understand? Why or why not?

Understanding

Gordon Dickson's story "3-Part Puzzle" (*The Star Road*) is about an
envoy from an alien race who tries to decipher the meaning of the
children's tale "The Three Billy Goats Gruff." To the envoy the obvious
and even tiresome military moral of the story seems clear. When the
smaller goats are faced with an enemy of superior might, the troll, they
delay the conflict until the third Billy Goat Gruff appears on the scene.

The envoy wonders why the children hearing the story laughed with
delight at the troll's fate. It may be a heroic story, even emotional, but

why did they feel delight instead of triumph? It is up to the envoy's superior to decipher the puzzle. The superior explains that what delighted the children about the tale of the Three Billy Goats Gruff is that it is a story about justice. There is such a thing as wrong and right, and we delight in the triumph of the right. Humans delight in justice and rejoice in the right. At least we'd like to think so. So often, however, human triumphs are tarnished. Innocent people suffer. Motives for winning are not purely just. And methods for overcoming an opponent are sometimes excessive.

Just wait, though. According to the apocalypticists, God's explosive return into history is going to be pure. "My boyfriend's back and you're gonna be sorry" runs the line in an oldies song. We could just as well chant, "Our God is back . . . ." If we just delay the conflict until God comes to take care of it, we too can rejoice in a victory over evil.

Daniel's vision of victory in chapter 8 is placed in the year 548/547 B.C., during the rule of Belshazzar, but it's set in Susa, the winter capital of the Persian kings, which was rebuilt around the year 552 B.C. To make matters more confusing, it resembles the events that followed the desecration of the Jewish temple by Antiochus IV Epiphanes in December 167 B.C. The Book of Daniel truly speaks to every age.

In the vision, Daniel sees two fearsome animals. First there is a ram with two horns, which will be revealed to be the kingdoms of Media and Persia. The ram is strong and has its way over other beasts, until a more powerful goat with a single horn vanquishes it. The goat represents the mighty conqueror Alexander the Great.

It's worth noting that in contrast to the animals of the previous vision, both the ram and the goat are clean, rather than unclean, animals. It's also important to mention that neither is under judgment for its acts. It's sort of like the old commercial for a cold remedy in which a sweeter than saccharine kid says, "Mothers are like that, yeah they are." One underlying message of this vision is that "Nations are like that, yeah they are."

The goat grows powerful, but eventually its great horn shatters, representing the death of Alexander, and four new horns emerge, representing the four generals commanding Alexander's kingdom. Then the vision gets personal for Daniel and his people. One of the small horns represents the Jews' old nemesis Antiochus IV Epiphanes (him again), and he prepares for battle not only against other beasts, but against the stars of the heavens, who we know from Judges 5:20 are God's faithful people. Here Daniel alludes to what is called the Abomination of Desolation when Antiochus's army overruns Jerusalem, killing and enslaving Jews, and eventually desecrating the temple by offering pagan sacrifices on the altar. God's people are persecuted and the sacrifices at the temple are halted. How long will the reign of this dreadful king last?

The answer to how long is "two thousand three hundred evenings and mornings" (8:14). That does not refer to 2300 days, as most assume, but to half that many. When the temple was shut down, offerings that would have been given in the morning and evening were curtailed, so counting one morning and evening as one day, the number of days works out to 1150. This is not quite three and a half years. Seven years in Hebrew numeration signifies a fulfilled time, and three and a half signifies a broken time. The message seems to be that the conqueror's time will be short and unfulfilled. This is indeed what happened, although neither 1150 nor 2300 equals the number of days the temple was shut down. The actual time according to 1 Maccabees was three years and ten days.

Daniel is not sure he understands what the vision means, but help is on the way in the form of one who looks like a man and is named Gabriel. Gabriel figures prominently in the New Testament as the one who announces to Mary that she will bear the coming Messiah. He also appears in many of the apocryphal books. Jewish legend describes him as the angel in charge of paradise, the one who guided Joseph to his brothers who were with the sheep, one of those who buried Moses, and one of those who defeated Sennacherib's army.

When Daniel realizes he is standing in the presence of an angel, he falls forward on his face in fear, a typical response in scripture to the presence of God's representatives. Gabriel explains the vision. The angel says of the deceitful king: "Without warning he shall destroy many and shall even rise up against the Prince of princes. But he shall be broken, and not by human hands" (8:25). The idea that this is God's battle, not a human one, is what convinced Daniel's readers to stand in opposition to the Maccabean philosophy of violent struggle. For the most part, the people were nonresistant. So like the previous chapters, the message to Daniel and his friends is that God is more powerful than human kings, and in his time he will vanquish the conquerors.

After Gabriel explains the vision, Daniel feels sick, and it is some days before he can resume his duties, but resume them he does. The message of this chapter seems to be that even when times are tough, we have to go about our daily lives. The thing that gets us through it all is the almost secret knowledge that God reigns and will rule.

Coded Messages

Although the message in this vision is similar to that of the previous chapter, there is one big difference. This vision is in Hebrew. It was for Daniel's people alone. Apocalyptic knowledge is secret knowledge not because it is hidden, but because the world refuses to understand it. God is shouting love at the heart of the world, but some are not willing to hear it.

The world speaks a different language and will not listen to the biblical message. The language of the world is dog-eat-dog; the one who dies with the most toys wins. That is part of the reason the rulers are portrayed as stubborn, brutish rams and goats. This is the way they act.

Our language, if we can consider ourselves on God's side, is the language of heaven, which others simply can't understand. As Paul puts it, "For the message about the cross is foolishness to those who are perishing, but to us who are being saved it is the power of God" (1 Cor. 1:18).

Another reason for composing this passage in Hebrew and using the symbols of a ram and a goat might have been to lessen the danger in spreading this word of encouragement. Since Antiochus was executing every circumcised man and child and anyone found with the Torah, it would have been suicidal to be openly critical of oppressive rulers. To speak in code was safer. Apocalyptic literature is often written in a code that is clear to the reader but not to the oppressor.

Revelation 18

The second reading for this week is another apocalyptic passage, but it is taken from the New Testament, not the Apocrypha. Apocalyptic literature is not found only in the Old Testament and the Apocrypha. It can be found in the New Testament in Mark 13, Matthew 24, Luke 21, 1 and 2 Thessalonians, and, of course, Revelation.

Revelation 18 is a song about the fall of Babylon. Just as Daniel uses code words to talk about Antiochus, the vision in Revelation uses Babylon to secretly represent Rome, the new oppressor. What Roman authority could object to reading about a long defeated nation? But the readers living under the oppressive rule of the Roman emperor knew that this was Rome. Rome or Babylon, the message is just as truthful.

This chapter of the Revelation to John is a chapter of retribution. Babylon finally gets her deserts. There has to be some satisfaction for the reader that justice finally reigns, especially when they apply the message to Rome. But are we ready to be victors in Christ? Most of the time we experience life from the perspective of the loser. What does it mean to be a good winner? Does the satisfaction in winning go to our heads? Is it possible to be too smug about winning? From my perspective defeat can be made a lot worse by poor winners, so when I've been on a winning team, I've been almost embarrassed and apologetic for having won.

But not always. I remember the many times I used to play hooky from seminary, running off with friends to see the White Sox play in the late seventies. There was a special taunt that fans used there, which later spread to other sports. It's the chorus from a pop song that goes, "Na, na, na, na, Na, na na, na, Hey, Hey, Goodbye!" We sang it over and over and over again when an opposing pitcher was lifted for a reliever, or when a hated opposing manager was thrown out of a game for arguing with a call. The purpose of the song was simple. Make a bad situation worse for a visiting team that was losing. Rub a little salt in the wounds.

But baseball is baseball and the end of the world is something else (though it was hard to tell the difference during the baseball strike). After a long tyranny is ended, the victors want to rejoice at oppression's demise, and Revelation's reminder that Babylon's days are numbered feels more like a cause for rejoicing than retribution.

Is it proper to feel so smug about the defeat of nations? Routing out oppression is a good thing, but God's people knew their defeat and exile into the hands of their oppressors were the direct result of their unfaithfulness in the first place. To the Hebrew mind, it was clear that the victory in 587 B.C., the beginning of the exile, did not belong to foreign gods and foreign armies. Nor was their defeat a defeat for God. All victory belonged to God. In the end, Israel was sure that just as they felt God's rod of justice, so would their oppressors in God's time.

We have seen the same action in recent years as some televangelists were brought low. To differing extents they had taken on the trappings of the world, making money the center of their ministries. Eventually their "sins" were found out and their self-serving ministries failed. It was not people, but God's judgment, that brought the proud low.

Maybe the biggest danger is that God's victory starts to feel like our victory, though most of us can probably claim very little credit. I remember the Christian comic books about Revelation that were passed around college when I was a student. I didn't have much patience for them. As far as I could tell from the drawings, all those caught up in the rapture were young and white. There were no older people, no ethnics. When people wanted justice, they wanted "just us," people who looked like them. It's too easy to think that we are equal to God. Whatever we want it what God wants.

What we've failed to see, however, is that even God's judgment and destruction can be a vehicle for salvation. Vernard Eller, in his book on Revelation, points out that while the kings of the world are the ultimate villains in the apocalyptic saga, they're also leading the parade in the heavenly city once the gates are opened. God's ways are mysterious, and there is no limit to the length God will go in order to save us and our supposed enemies.

In the meantime we should remember that God is in control of history. And there will always be those who assault heaven, but this too shall pass.

> Upon the plain of Meggido they gather.
> The scimitars are flashing in the sun.
> The clouds presage a change is in the weather
> And soon the days of conflict will be done.
> Prepared in rage to overwhelm the Lamb
> And his assembled saints from ages called,
> To, if they may, tear tendon, heart and limb,
> And burn to bitumen the heaven's walls.
> They charge. Is Babylon triumphant,
> Her standard raised, her princes grim arrayed,
> With martyrs' trophied skulls ascendant,
> No end in sight their rule of sun and shade?
> Nay. As the waves are spent against the shore,
> They roil and retreat, are seen no more.
> —F. Ramirez

Discussion and Action

1. Share some of the battles going on in your lives. Which ones really belong to God and which ones are yours to deal with? How difficult is it to give battles over to God? Give each other ideas for how to be patient as you wait.

2. Walt Kelly's comic strip character, *Pogo*, once said, "We have met the enemy and he is us." Who is the "enemy" today? In what ways are we our own worst enemies? How is our culture like Babylon? What response should we have to the warnings in today's readings?

3. Evangelists encourage us to tell others about God's love, but if, according to the texts for this session, the world can't understand God's ways, are we wasting our breath? Who should we tell the good news to? What should we say?

4. As a group, devise a list of criteria for judging which side you're on in a conflict. Your list should help you tell to the best of your ability that you are on God's side. It should help you be sure you are not just serving yourself or assuming that what you want is what God wants. Try out these steps in a situation, such as a conflict in the congregation, a hot community issue, or national issues affecting Christians.

5. Share with the group your most significant victory. Then share your most significant loss. Tell how you felt after both incidents. Where was God in both your victory and your defeat?

6. What situation in the world today is our modern Babylon? Create an apocalyptic acrostic with the word *Babylon*. Use words that begin with each letter of the word *Babylon* to describe an oppressive situation today and how you hope God will resolve it. For example, describe racism:

    Black skin prejudice.
    Asian prejudice.
    Brown skin prejudice.
    Yearly statistics on hate crimes against people of color.
    Living together is difficult.
    Only God has the solution—
    New life comes in Christ who came for all.

7. Israelites in exile had to face the fact that they suffered because they were unfaithful. How much suffering in the world is the result of our own misbehavior and how much is truly unwarranted? How long should we be expected to repent for the sins of our ancestors for holding slaves, for instance, or taking land away from people living on the land? How can these old conflicts be resolved?

8. Who are the oppressors now who will be leading the way in the apocalypse? If God can be reconciled to these people, can you also be reconciled to them? Why or why not?

9

Daniel's Prayer for the People
Daniel 9; Baruch 4:21-29

Like Daniel and Baruch, we must finally face the fact that kings are not the only unholy, unfaithful people. We have also failed God. We are God's enemies. How will we repent? How will God respond?

Personal Preparation

1. Read Daniel 9 and Baruch 4:21-29. Daniel prays by himself but says "we." As you pray this week, pray as "we." What confession can you as a family, a congregation, or a group make? What prayers of thanksgiving or praise can you make?
2. Recall stories of deathbed conversions or the stories of people who confessed or repented under pressure. How do you know their confessions are authentic? Do you think they deserve forgiveness? Why or why not?
3. Under what circumstances has someone prayed for you? How does it feel to have someone else praying on your behalf? What were they praying about? What did God's answer seem to be?

Understanding

A good friend of mine taught a religion course at a time when there was a national upsurge in religious enthusiasm. By definition, the student's zeal for the topic was accompanied by a complete intolerance for any view but their own. This friend told me that once in a while, after he gave a lecture in class, some of the students would make a great show of bowing their heads to pray for him and his errors.

What irritated him about the students' prayers was that they always started from a perspective of righteousness, as if the students had never sinned. In this chapter, Daniel's prayer starts from the opposite perspective. He, one of God's favorites, has come to confess his sins when he prays for himself and the sins of the people as well.

In this week's chapter, Daniel writes as one of the exiles who has outlived the Babylonians, but not the exile. In 538 B.C., under the reign of the Chaldeans, Daniel wonders how long his people will live in bondage, so he sets his mind on the prophecies of Jeremiah. He reflects on God's message to Jeremiah that the exile will last seventy years. The relevant passages in Jeremiah read: "This whole land shall become a ruin and a waste, and these nations shall serve the king of Babylon seventy years. Then after seventy years are completed, I will punish the king of Babylon and that nation, the land of the Chaldeans, for their iniquity, says the LORD, making the land an everlasting waste" (Jer. 25:11-12), and "For thus says the LORD: Only when Babylon's seventy years are completed will I visit you, and I will fulfill to you my promise and bring you back to this place" (Jer. 29:10). And indeed, Jeremiah's seventy years is a very good approximation of the period between the fall of Jerusalem and the restoration of God's people to the land.

Why seventy years? Because it's a multiple of seven, and seven was understood as a unique sort of number, standing on its own, indivisible, yet an integral part of many other numbers. Seven meant completeness. It was used many times in scripture. The writer of 2 Chronicles, for instance, thought the seventy years of the nation's ruin comprised a sabbath for the 490 years of Israelite monarchy, in which God's people turned away from the covenant.

But Daniel wants to meditate further. Just as we look back to the original context of a scripture passage to discover how it is speaking to us today, Daniel wants to explore what God's message to the exiles years before might mean to those undergoing persecution during the time of the Maccabees. Does this scripture have meaning for the period of time between 167 and 164 B.C., when temple worship was interrupted by another cruel oppressor? Would the people have to wait seventy years after Anitiochus for temple worship to be restored, or was there another way to look at these numbers?

Daniel's approach to scripture study begins with prayer, as should ours. That he turns to prayer should not be surprising. Daniel is consistently a man of prayer. Before he ventured to interpret Nebuchadnezzar's dream in chapter 2, he gathered together other believers to form a community of prayer. And in chapter 6 he refuses to give up his faithful practice of prayer even though it puts his life in danger.

Without question God is ready to hear the prayers of anyone, regardless of their past or whether they've prayed continually throughout their trouble. Indeed, the parables of the Lost Sheep and the Lost Coin make it clear that God seems to pay special attention to the one who has wandered furthest from the fold. You may know an individual whose testimony includes a desperate prayer after years of ignoring God. That may even be your own confession. These prayers are just as valid as the prayers of the most disciplined person.

It is never too late to turn to God in prayer. Jesus promised the thief on the cross they would meet that day in paradise. There is always the hope of a new beginning. The psalmist says, "Create in me a clean heart, O God, and put a new and right spirit within me" (Ps. 51:10). "Forgive us our debts," Jesus admonishes us to pray, "as we forgive our debtors," emphasizing that forgiveness on God's part leads us to forgive others. Even in nonbiblical writings, we read of God's endless willingness to listen to belated prayers. In Dante's "Purgatorio," the second part of his epic poem *The Divine Comedy*, a character named Belacqua is saved even though he waits until the last second to pray.

It is not God's faithfulness that is in question here, but our own spiritual muscle. Just like exercise, it's easier to turn to God in prayer if we do it regularly. I have seen people who sign up for a five- or ten-kilometer run the morning of a race and successfully run it without any training. But the next day their aching muscles ensure they won't take up training or make running a regular part of their lives. By contrast, those who walk or run a short distance each day, gradually increasing the time and distance they run, go on to make exercise a regular part of their regimen. In the same way, people who have built up their endurance in prayer little by little each day can condition their prayer muscles until much of their day is spent in communion with God, speaking, confessing, confiding, rejoicing.

When we come to God in prayer is a lot less important than how we come. Our prayer should not be offered from a self-righteous position, but from a stance of humility in our unworthiness and trust in God's mercy. Daniel confesses his own sins and the sins of his people and makes it clear that he does not come before God as one who has a right to expect God's deliverance. Instead, his confession is an admission of how much God's people rely on him and how much they have failed.

Daniel's prayer is preceded by fasting. Bible characters do not fast because the things of this world are evil and they are trying to avoid them. In fact, scripture has a high view of the created world. God declared that all these things were good. Fasting is a way to focus the mind and the heart. Wait an hour longer for your next meal and notice how alert you are. Then imagine training all your thought of food on prayer.

In later biblical tradition, fasting and prayer are the prelude to battle. And for Daniel all battle is spiritual battle, not physical. Notice that Daniel is never involved in any violent struggle. Every episode is a struggle of faith. In every case Daniel shows that nonviolent resistance is a powerful means of resisting tyrants. The real quarrel is not between us and the tyrants, however, but between God and the tyrants; and the visions and stories of Daniel make it clear who will be the victor.

Just As I Am

Daniel's confession on behalf of the people admits that they have rejected the prophets in years past. He acknowledges that the people are not worthy of any further prophetic enlightenment, but, he says, "We do not present our supplication before you on the ground of our righteousness, but on the ground of your great mercies" (9:18b). As the Charlotte Elliot hymn puts it, "Just as I am, without one plea, but that thy blood was shed for me, and that thou bidst me come to thee . . . ." Confession opens the door for our approach to the throne of God.

The confession of sin is important. C. S. Lewis once noted that forgiving a sin was different than excusing it. We tend to want to have our sins excused rather than confess them and have them forgiven. But when we can't confess them, we cut off the possibility of real forgiveness.

Confession and forgiveness are real opportunities. Not long ago the Southern Baptist Convention made a public confession that they had wrongfully taken part in oppression of African Americans and segregation of the races over the years. Their admission opened the door for forgiveness and healing of broken relationships between them and Baptists of color. But those Christians who rationalize the past sins of the church as another generation's problem can never really know true forgiveness from their brothers and sisters in Christ. When hate-filled criminals torched black churches in the mid-1990s, black church leaders were not always willing to accept help rebuilding their churches from members of white churches who had abandoned them in the days of slavery and later during segregation and the civil rights struggle. On the other hand, doors were open for the genuine support of Christians with whom they were reconciled.

On another front, fifty years after World War II, some Japanese Americans who were interned in camps during the war and their former neighbors met to be reconciled. The government has also apologized and provided restitution to Japanese Americans. Neighbors have confessed they failed to stand up for the civil rights of their fellow citizens, and for the first time, deep wounds have begun to heal.

Daniel wants this kind of healing for the bumbling people of God. As Daniel prays he recalls God's saving history, including the dramatic exodus from Egypt, even though it means calling to mind as well the disobedience in the desert. This leads to a final confession and a plea for God's forgiveness and action. The response is quick. "While I was speaking in prayer, the man Gabriel, whom I had seen before in a vision, came to me in swift flight" (9:21).

Angels We Have Heard on High

The arrival of an angel in scripture always fills me with delight and a little frustration because the descriptions are so sparse. We know very little of their comings and goings. That's probably why I enjoy a book like *This Present Darkness* by Frank Peretti, where the reader is transported to a world of angels. Even though the story is a human creation, I like to imagine that this is really how angels operate.

I suspect we know so little of angels for a couple of important reasons. First of all, it's none of our business what they're doing. Secondly, I'm not sure we'd understand most of it even if we tried. It's like being a child again when we didn't understand certain aspects of the adult life around us. We took everything at face value then, like my younger son who once insisted he wear shorts on a very cold day. He noticed when he wore shorts it was hot, so he hoped to change the temperature by his style of dress. Making sense of angels wouldn't be any easier.

God answers prayer, and in this case the answer consists of an explanation from an angel that is both clear and obscure. What is clear in the message is that time is running out for the one who is causing all the difficulties for God's people. When his time comes, he's going to get whatever he gave out. Once again, as in much of the book, the thinly veiled reference is to Antiochus IV Epiphanes.

The New Math

Gabriel's reply is about as obvious as VCR instructions. He is trying to describe how it will take seventy years to complete the exile. It's as if each day is a year and each week is seven years. Therefore, the seventy weeks before the temple will be restored is more like seventy-times-seven years, or 490 years. If a week is equal to seven years, then as Gabriel reveals, Antiochus will disrupt worship in the temple for less than a week, or three and a half years.

On one hand 490 years doesn't work out quite right. The actual period of time from Daniel's prayer to the death of Antiochus was about 430 years. If we push it back to Jeremiah's reckoning, it comes to 441. On the other hand, the three and a half years of trouble from Antiochus is about perfect.

The mathematical accuracy of either calculation is immaterial. It's not the quantity but the quality of the numbers that matters in the Bible. Seven is a number that signifies completeness or wholeness. Seventy years in this instance expresses the idea that a period of penance had drawn to a close and seventy-times-seven is a sign of completion. By contrast, three and a half signifies that a period of time has been cut short. God's people will see that when the time is complete God's power will be displayed and God's sovereignty over history will be made apparent. Conversely, earthly tyrants who usurp God's place should know that, despite their best plans, their time will be cut short.

Daniel believes that the Antiochan persecution is about to end and includes Gabriel's calculation as evidence that a divinely ordained period of 490 years is drawing to a close. He is not trying to predict anything. He is trying to describe what is happening. Any attempt to use multiples of seven and complicated equations for calendarizing the end of the world will never work.

In 1987 I received a free book in the mail called *88 Reasons the World Will End in 1988*. Believe it or not, a little over a year later, when the world was still in one piece, I got another free book explaining why the first book was wrong and why there was every reason to expect that 1989 or 1990 would be the year of Jesus' return. Only this time the author was sure. Honest.

The Hal Lindseys of this world will never go broke publishing new books of end time predictions. No one seems to hold them accountable; no one cares that these forecasters are wrong again and again and again.

Numerologists will gain no benefit from Daniel—or Revelation—if they come at it with a calculator. These are numbers that speak to our hearts and not to our heads. Or as Bible scholar John Goldingay puts it so very well: "The period of deepest oppression did last about three and a half years, but that is not the point. This is not prognostication or prediction. It is promise."

Baruch

Baruch is a short book in the Apocrypha attributed to Jeremiah's secretary and friend. According to Jeremiah 43:1-7, Baruch was deported to Egypt with the prophet Jeremiah in 582 B.C., but Baruch's letter was written at about the same time from exile in Babylon to the priests and people of Jerusalem. There is little point in trying to rectify the historical errors in the book, however, because it is not likely that this book was even written by Baruch. It was probably written at a much later date, perhaps 150 B.C. Portions of it may be even newer.

The first readers of Baruch may have known that the book's author was not actually the friend of Jeremiah, but they would not have considered the work a fraud. It was a literary tradition of the time that books be named after a worthy person of the past, in recognition that what was true in a bygone era is true now.

The book consists largely of prayers. Major portions of it are derived from scripture. Baruch 1:15–2:19, for example, looks a lot like Daniel 9:4-19. Again, the ancients found no problem in patterning their prayers and writings on the works of others. In the twentieth century, we sometimes labor too hard under the belief that all our prayers should be totally original. Indeed, some people have a prejudice against written prayers, going so far as to say that written prayers denote a lack of faith in the Spirit. We know all too well, however, that spontaneous prayers can be repetitious and banal.

Whether written by Baruch himself or by an author using his name, these prayers are like the prayers Daniel prays on behalf of the people. Baruch simultaneously prays a prayer of confession for the sins of the people and offers prayers of praise for God's faithfulness.

Baruch's use of some of Daniel's language, rearranged slightly, is a tribute to the prophet and a reminder that the true author of our prayer is rightly God. As C. S. Lewis writes in his poem "Prayer":

> . . . I seek in myself the things I meant to say
> And lo the wells are dry.
>
> Then, seeing me empty, you forsake
> The Listener's role, and through
> My dead lips breathe and into utterance wake
> The thoughts I never new.
> —from *Poems*, 122-123

Baruch's prayers contain assurances that God will in time ease the suffering of the people and restore them for his name's sake. "My children, endure with patience the wrath that has come upon you from God," Baruch writes in 4:25. "For the one who brought these calamities upon you will bring you everlasting joy with your salvation" (4:29).

God's answers come when the time is right. Our response in the meantime should be faithfulness. Recently, a church member told me how he and his wife had begun praying for a good friend about whom they were concerned. It was their hope that God would make a change in this friend's life. The church member told me that after thirty years of faithful prayer their friend was baptized. Their own personal "seventy years" was complete—forty years early. But then, it's not the quantity, it's the quality that matters.

Daniel prays for the people. To feel prayed for can be a royal annoyance, or it can be a special blessing. When we pray for others as a way to make them look pitiful and ourselves righteous, we have removed God to the sidelines in the whole matter. But to hear someone pray for another in times of trouble can be a special balm of blessedness. "I'll remember you in prayer" can be the most important words ever spoken by a Christian.

Discussion and Action

1. When God is the author of prayer through us, what does God pray for? How do you know when it is you praying and when it is God praying through you?

2. For which of your prayers have you not received an answer yet? Share ideas for how you keep up the discipline of prayer when it seems hopeless.

3. What has been your attitude about praying for the seemingly impossible, such as world peace or the end of suffering? What does it mean to each of you to be faithful as you wait for the fullness of time or the answer to prayer?

4. Recite Psalm 51 together as a group. What part does confession play in prayers for peace or the end of suffering. What could you confess in your prayers for peace? What prayers of thanksgiving for peace can you give to God?

5. What is prayer to you? What forms does your prayer take?

6. Tell about a time someone prayed for you. How did you feel about it? Was it welcomed or unwelcomed? Why? Who needs your prayers now? Privately decide who to pray for and decide whether you should let them know you are praying for them.

7. Look in an almanac or encyclopedia at what was happening 490 years ago. What injustices have been righted over time? What evils were interrupted because they could not last? Close with sentence prayers for God's faithfulness in these situations.

10

Happy Are Those Who Persevere
Daniel 10–12; The Book of Tobit

The angel Michael shows Daniel that heaven and earth are connected, that our battles are like the larger cosmic struggle between good and evil. In those battles, God is the winner. There is no one like God. This is the message of hope for God's people on earth.

Personal Preparation

1. Read Daniel 10–12 and the Book of Tobit. Examine your life to see if you are overly conscious of time or basically unaware of time. As people of faith, how should we regard time? Important? Unimportant? Why?
2. What are angels? How are angels different from God? When, if ever, have you had an encounter with an angel?
3. How has your thinking changed about apocalypse in the Bible? What remains mysterious about it? How do the apocalyptic writings in the Bible give you hope?

Understanding

Rumors are more powerful than truth and can be difficult to eradicate. In our modern era, there are many famous rumors that have been proven false, but which people have come to accept as true. In most cases they are harmless stories, like the belief that if your Tootsie Roll candy wrapper displays an Indian pointing his arrow at the moon, you will get a free Tootsie Roll.

Other stories are costly. Procter & Gamble, a major producer of household cleaners and soaps, lost sales revenue and spent lots of money to combat rumors that its logo of moon and stars is some sort of satanic symbol. The Federal Communications Commission, which regulates television in the United States, has had to handle hundreds of thousands of petitions from worried TV viewers who have heard that an atheist is going to block all religious programming on television. And the makers of Snapple beverages has gone to some lengths to counteract the rumor that its logo depicts a slave galley. These defensive measures cost companies—and consumers—lots of money.

Costly rumors have also plagued Christianity. At the end of the first century of Christianity, rumors abounded about those odd followers of Jesus. Popular stories depicted Christians as cannibals who practiced incest and infant sacrifice.

To dispel these rumors, Christians wrote tracts, telling the truth about Christianity. One of the best, and earliest, is the anonymous "Letter to Diognetus," written during the first half of the second Christian century. Among the things written in this letter are sentences that aptly describe the place of the believer in the world.

> For Christians are not distinguished from the rest of humanity by country, language, or custom. For nowhere do they live in cities of their own, nor do they speak some unusual dialect, nor do they practice an eccentric lifestyle. . . . But while they live in both Greek and barbarian cities, as each one's lot was cast, and follow the local customs in dress and food and other aspects of life, at the same time they demonstrate the remarkable and admittedly unusual character of their own citizenship. They live in their own countries, but only as aliens; they participate in everything as citizens, and endure everything as foreigners. . . . They live on earth, but their citizenship is in heaven. . . . They love everyone, and by everyone they are persecuted. . . . They are put to death, yet they are brought to life.

The tract lists several customs, such as disposing of unwanted children or sharing spouses, which Christians do not take part in, but adds that "they are poor, yet they make many rich; they are in need of everything, yet they abound in everything."

Reality consists of two components, that which is seen and that which is unseen. The believer knows that the unseen is often more powerful than the seen. Rumors, even though they are false, can be just as real as the truth. At the same time, the truth is also unseen and sometimes hard to believe. We profess with all we're worth that God will re-enter history in a dramatic fashion and bring down the curtain on sin's legacy. But if we're honest, we have to say we don't really know the details of how this will come to pass.

That's okay. Since we don't know when or how Jesus will return, we have to be prepared all the time. It's like a student whose teacher gives pop quizzes now and then. The student has to be ready each day. If we knew the whens and the wheres, we would probably be more like the student who knows the date for the final exam and doesn't bother to really study until the night before. It's human nature.

Jesus, in answering questions from his disciples about the end times, pointed out that if the householder knew when a thief was coming, he'd have been ready. His parable of the Bridesmaids, half of whom failed to have enough oil for their lamps and thus missed the ceremony they'd been waiting for, gives the same message. Better to always be prepared.

This last prophecy of the Book of Daniel, contained in chapters ten through twelve, seems at first reading to give a detailed time map that if properly deciphered would unlock the key to the end times. But in reality, nothing could be further from the truth.

If you believe that these chapters of the Book of Daniel were written right after the Babylonian exile, as suggested in the first couple of verses of chapter ten, then these chapters contain the most accurate biblical prophecy ever written. On the other hand, considering the number of historical inaccuracies in the description of the Babylonian captivity and the extraordinary accuracy of the details when applied to the Maccabean history, one might ask why Daniel can see so clearly into the future and so dimly in the present. There is roughly a one-to-one correspondence between the symbols of the vision and historical events from the time of Alexander the Great through Antiochus IV Epiphanes (the "contemptible person on whom royal majesty has not been conferred" in Daniel 11:21).

What historical events correspond to the vision? The typical boring intrigues of kings. Three or four pages of the vision correspond to various Seleucids (the kings of the north) and the Ptolemies (the kings of the south) and their dismal exploits and alliances. You would meet Ptolemies I-VI and Seleucids I-IV, as well as the various kings named Antiochus, and learn about all their battles and conquests.

Conversely, you might decide that this part of Daniel was written during the time of Antiochus IV Epiphanes and that the prophecy *ex eventu* (prophecy written after the fact) is an historian's way of recording the events that had already occurred.

It doesn't matter. The meaning is still the same. "Happy are those who persevere and attain the thousand three hundred and thirty-five days" (12:12). Or the "one thousand two hundred and ninety days" (12:11). As mentioned earlier biblical numbers are not so much concerned with quantity as quality. It's not the precise number of days that's important; it's that the number of days is short. Both numbers represent three and a half years, which, as mentioned earlier, refer to a broken time, a time cut short and unfulfilled. The Babylonian year, based on the phases of the moon, was 354 days. The Essenes, a Jewish sect, used a calendar based on the movement of the sun across the sky that was 364 days, and the Greek world used a calendar of 360 days, combining features of the lunar and solar calendars. All three calendars used special days or months to bring the total to the actual length of the year: 365 ¼ days (1290 days = 3 ½ lunar years; 1335 days is 3 ½ solar years).

This time of trial inflicted on Jews at the hands of Antiochus was three and a half years, but since, according to 1 Maccabees, the period between the Abomination of Desolation when the temple was profaned and its rededication by the Jews was exactly three years, you can see that the number of three and a half years is meant to be symbolic. It is meant to show that the rule of any oppressor will be cut short. This is God's message through God's word to God's people.

Those who match the events of the last vision with the period of the Maccabees are right, at least historically. But those who see our own time reflected in these words are also correct, provided they don't use this vision to date the end with precision. No matter what the details are, the message is the same for those taken away to Babylon, for those who suffered under Antiochus, for those who felt the wrath of Nero or Domitian, for those who were persecuted by religious authorities during the Radical Reformation, for those who suffer for their faith today. It's a message that has been reiterated time and again in this book. Be faithful, be watchful, be patient, be loving. Do not take up the weapons of this world, but resist with love and nonviolence and God will deliver the people in God's time.

Part of the encouragement in this chapter is that we are not alone in this struggle. There are unseen forces; there are angels. When things are at their worst Michael will rise. Who are these angels? Why don't we know more about them? How do they work? The word for angel, in both Hebrew and Greek, means messenger. What does that tell us?

A friend of mine told me an angel story once. As a utility worker, he was called out to work after the Palm Sunday tornado wreaked havoc in Elkhart, Indiana. It was his job to turn off the gas lines at a number of damaged homes. There was no telling if any of them would blow. He was nervous and worried about his life and the welfare of his family. He felt exposed and alone as he went from place to place.

Suddenly there was another man with him. The man didn't identify himself but said he could help; he accompanied my friend while he went about his work, providing calm assurance and the feeling that he wasn't alone. This man stayed with my friend until the work was done, and just as suddenly he wasn't there anymore.

This is my kind of angel story: practical help in times of trouble, the visible manifestation of God's love, comfort that encourages human action, and just enough ambiguity that you can't build up a solid angelology to convince the skeptics—because the purpose of angels is not to prove anything. Sometimes the angel seems to be God's way of expressing himself. Other times angels seem to have entirely separate identities from God's. Their exact nature and purpose is left largely unexplained. There is no systematic angelology in the scriptures. But angels are there, and it would be as big a mistake to disbelieve in angels as it would be to worship them.

Angelology has become something of a fad in recent years. In a sense it is safe theology. We're not talking about God here, a Creator who makes demands and has the right to do so. Angels can just appear, do good deeds, and get out of the way when it's time to eat ice cream.

Nevertheless, angels have a place in creation. They are servants just like us. In this passage Michael is revealed as one who takes the part of God's people in a larger cosmic struggle. He appears in a similar context in Revelation 12, one of my favorite passages of scripture: "And war broke out in heaven" (7), with Michael and the dragon fighting each other. The dragon "was thrown down to the earth and his angels were thrown down with him" (Rev. 12:9).

The dragon is Satan, but that means that Revelation reports Satan's fall after the birth of Jesus. The fall of Satan, the brightest of the angels, is also described in Isaiah 14:12-14 and Ezekiel 28:11-17, long before Jesus. In the middle of his ministry, Jesus himself said, "I saw Satan fall from heaven like a flash of lightning" (Luke 10:18), while right before the crucifixion he said, "Now is the judgment of this world, now the ruler of this world will be driven out" (John 12:31). When did the fall of Lucifer occur? Was it in ages past? before the dawn of time on earth?

The chronology of the fall of Lucifer, like the chronology of Daniel and Revelation, remains a problem only if we insist on thinking about eternity in chronological terms. The question of when Satan was thrust from heaven is meaningless in chronological terms. If it happened in eternity, the event can be described with equal accuracy from the perspective of the past, the present, and the future.

Portions of scripture that deal with the end of time, such as Revelation 12 and Daniel 12, are themselves timeless, because they involve glimpses into eternity. Any attempt to pin down the date of Christ's return and the coming of the kingdom will fail if tied to a human perception of time.

Tobit

Perseverance, the prime virtue in the Book of Daniel, is also central to the delightful folktale Tobit in the Apocrypha. Three different characters persevere and are in the end rewarded. The actions of the angel Raphael and of the little dog make this both a cosmic and earthy story.

Tobit carries out God's will with regard to the burial of the dead and is condemned—he loses everything, even his sight. He is so crushed by circumstances that he nearly despairs and begs for release from life. He even contemplates suicide but is eventually vindicated. This does not happen overnight, however. Most of us can relate to how hard it is to take the long view in times of real trouble, for in the midst of a problem, vindication at some future time seems unlikely.

The tale of Tobit combines two strains of folktales, that of the Grateful Dead and that of the Unfortunate Bride. Grateful Dead folktales tell of the good fortune that comes to those who give strangers a proper burial. In this case, Tobit sees to the burial of Israelites taken away to Ninevah, their corpses thrown outside the city wall. As for the Unfortunate Bride theme, a virtuous young woman finds that her suitors are killed by an evil spirit. An adventurer must kill the spirit, and Tobias, son of Tobit, is the adventurer who saves her.

In this apocryphal book, the angel Raphael travels with Tobias, directing Tobias to cast out a demon and heal his father. With Raphael's help, Tobias wins a bride and restores fortune to the family. And while the angel seems to do a lot of the work, all of it would have come to nothing except that Tobias was willing to perform the tasks set for him. Part of the message seems to be that even with angelic help, we must take some initiative. Even with the knowledge that God will make all things new in the end, we have to help bring about at least a shadow of the kingdom.

This is the philosophy of Heifer Project International, a program begun shortly after World War II, that provides livestock to poor farmers all over the world. The only condition attached to this gift of hope is that farmers must pass along an offspring of the cow, sheep, or goat to another poor family. These recipients of God's good gifts must participate in the redemptive act somehow. Habitat for Humanity and its practice of "sweat equity" is another example of a group that takes initiative for a little part of the kingdom.

The Limits of Evil

In every age, there are rulers who seem so powerful, almost immovable. But each bully out there eventually encounters a bigger bully. Prior to his invasion of Judea, Antiochus IV Epiphanes had turned his sights on Egypt. He considered himself a great conqueror, a king born of a great line of kings.

But as we learn in Daniel 11:30, "Ships of Kittim shall come against him, and he shall lose heart and withdraw." Kittim is a code word for Rome and is the only reference to the burgeoning Roman empire in the Old Testament. Even as Antiochus besieged Alexandria in Egypt, an envoy from Rome was being dispatched to demand his withdrawal. The envoy drew a circle around Antiochus, the self-proclaimed image of God, and demanded a response before Antiochus stepped out of the ring. Faced with the armed might of Rome, Antiochus was forced to flee Egypt. He was humiliated and angry. Looking for his next target, he turned his rage against Jerusalem, invading in 168 B.C. Three and a half years later, however, that reign of terror also ended.

Given enough time, those who live by the sword will die by the sword. But those who live by faith in God triumph. Daniel stands as a testament to this fact and as an example of the endurance the faithful need to outlast evildoers. Jews and Christians suffering under evil regimes over the centuries have looked to Daniel for strength to endure and have hope for the future.

The Book of Daniel and various books of the Apocrypha were written during an exciting time (Lord preserve us from exciting times!) when the faith and practice of believers stood them in direct opposition to the world. Some responded to oppression with the sword; some responded by giving in to the ways of the world. But God's message through Daniel is that believers must endure, not passively but actively, speaking the truth to power, as the Quakers say. His message from beginning to end remains the same. Hold on! God is in control! His will shall be done on earth as it is in heaven—in God's time.

Discussion and Action

1. How would you define an angel? Can humans be angels? Are angels divine? Tell about your experiences with angels, or share the experiences of someone you know who has had an encounter with an angel.

2. Use a watch with a second hand and time each person as they talk about their attitudes toward time. Give each person one minute. How conscious are you of time? Why do you think you are either impatient for God to act or comfortable waiting for something to happen in God's time?

3. What will the world look like when God's will is done on earth as it is in heaven? How can you bring about at least a little of this in our time? Consider signing up as a group to work on a Habitat for Humanity project in your area or some other effort to bring in a little piece of the kingdom.

4. Think of times when God intervened, but the people didn't know it at the time. What, if any, are the signs that God is at work in a situation, even the most desperate situation? Why do you think God "allows" situations to become so desperate?

5. If the stories of Daniel are eternal and applicable to every age, where can the message of endurance be applied today for you personally? for your congregation? for your community? for the world?

6. What evidence do you see that evil is limited, that evil always fails in the end?

7. Though you may not be interested in predicting the day of apocalypse, the day and hour when God's kingdom will come, how do you stay prepared? Share ideas for how you can be ready in your daily life for the kingdom of God to arrive.

8. What authority do the writings of the Apocrypha have for you after studying some of them? Why would you or wouldn't you call them scriptures? Which ones are most meaningful to you?

9. How have your ideas about the apocalypse changed since studying Daniel? Close with sentence prayers that begin, "For me, the apocalypse is . . . ."

Suggestions for Sharing and Prayer

This material is designed for covenant groups that spend one hour sharing and praying together, followed by one hour of Bible study. The following suggestions will help relate the group's sharing and prayer time to their study of the Book of Daniel. Ideally, groups will use this opportunity to share with one another at an increasing depth as the weeks pass. Session-by-session ideas as well as several general resources for sharing and praying are provided in the following pages.

This section was written by Bill Robey, pastor of First Christian Church (Disciples of Christ) in Sumner, Washington.

Structure for Sharing and Prayer Time

Check-in Time: Spend about ten minutes talking about significant events or issues in your lives since you last met. Ensure that each person has the opportunity to check in and that no one dominates the whole time.

Centering: After check-in, assume a comfortable sitting position without arms or legs crossed. Begin playing peaceful, meditative music (see suggestions on page 93) and close your eyes. Inhale slowly to a count of five, filling your lungs with air. With your lungs full, hold for a count of five, then slowly and completely exhale to a count of five. Keep your lungs empty for a count of five, then repeat the cycle again. While inhaling, imagine you are breathing in God's Spirit, peace, comfort, and presence. While exhaling, breathe out your worldly concerns, troubles, and worries. Continue this exercise for at least five minutes.

Holy Imaging: While still in the centering position, bring to mind the particular image suggested for each week in the session-by-session suggestions. Have someone read aloud the Holy Imaging paragraph to the group, allowing time between suggestions to dwell on each. After three to five minutes, open your eyes and re-enter the group setting.

Holy Reflecting: Once everyone is back in the group, share what you experienced during the Holy Imaging time, using the questions provided in the session-by-session suggestions. If you have a large group (eight or more), you might want to pair off for this part. Spend about five minutes in Holy Reflecting.

Other Sharing Activities: Each session will include two or three other ideas for sharing. Choose those that most fit your group, or bring your own ideas. Plan to spend about fifteen minutes with these activities.

Prayer Time: Begin a prayer list during your first session. Each week review, update, add, and delete individuals and situations on the list. Through this exercise, be aware of God's activity in the life of your group and in the lives of those you uphold in prayer, remembering that God's silence in a situation is also a response to prayer. Spend about twenty minutes for prayer.

Closing Hymn: Close the sharing and prayer time by singing the suggested hymn. If you do not have a particularly musical group, recite the words of the hymn in unison or in some other creative way.

1. Enduring Together

Check-in Time: Begin this first check-in time by forming or renewing your covenant together. Use the Litany of Commitment on page 93, or develop your own covenant for the next ten weeks. Use any remaining time to highlight important happenings in your lives since your last meeting.

Centering

Holy Imaging: In John 14:2, Jesus says, "I go to prepare a place for you." Picture yourself moving toward a difficult place or dilemma that you are facing right now or in the near future, or that you have faced in the past. [*pause*] Now picture Jesus joining you as you move toward that dilemma. Walk with him for a few moments. [*pause*] What does he say to you? [*pause*] How do you respond? [*pause*] How does this make you feel? [*pause*] Jesus is leaving you now. What does he have to say to you in parting? [*pause*] Open your eyes, look around, become present in this place, and slowly rejoin the group.

Holy Reflecting: In pairs or as a whole group, talk about the difficult places or dilemmas you are facing if you can. What did Jesus have to say to you in your holy image? How did you respond? Will Jesus' words help you through this difficult time? If so, how and why? If not, why not?

Other Sharing Activities

❑ Find a copy of the classic Uncle Remus story *Brer Rabbit and the Tar-Baby* by Joel Chandler Harris. (Your local library should have this readily available.) Assign members of your group to be the various characters in the story, and have fun reading it as a group. How did this story give encouragement to those who were suffering under the yoke of slavery?

❑ What nicknames did you have as a child? How did you get your nickname? Why did you like or dislike being called by your nickname?

❑ Read Psalm 137 together. As you read, imagine the feelings of those who witnessed the destruction of their most sacred shrine and then went into exile in a strange and distant land. Has anything ever happened to you that elicited these same feelings? Do you believe the desire for vindication expressed in verse 9 is justified? Why or why not?

❑ Describe the first time you were away from family and friends for an extended time. How did you feel? What helped you to adjust to being alone in a strange place?

❑ Where do you see God's rules in conflict with the world's rules today? What do you believe is the cause of these conflicts? What can your covenant group do to help resolve these conflicts?

Prayer Time: Begin your prayer list during this session. Once the list is complete, say sentence prayers on behalf of each name on the list.

Closing Hymn: Sing together or read the verses of the African American spiritual "Lift Every Voice and Sing."

2. Speaking the Truth, No Matter What

Check-in Time: Check in with the group and share any significant happenings or issues that have been part of your life during the past week.

Centering

Holy Imaging: In John 8, Jesus says, "If you continue in my word, you are truly my disciples; and you will know the truth, and the truth will make you free." For today's holy image, try to remember a time in your life when you did not tell the truth. [*pause*] Picture in your mind the people and the circumstances surrounding that incident. [*pause*] Remember how you felt afterward. [*pause*] Now imagine yourself approaching Jesus, confessing your part in this incident, and receiving his forgiveness. [*pause*] What does Jesus say to you? What are you asked to do? [*pause*] How do you respond? [*pause*] How does this make you feel? [*pause*] Open your eyes, look around, become present in this place, and slowly rejoin the group.

Holy Reflecting: In pairs or in the larger group, share as much of your holy imaging as is comfortable. How did confessing the truth to Jesus make you feel about the incident that came to mind? How was this a "freeing" experience? How do you feel compelled to respond to Jesus' forgiveness?

Other Sharing Activities

❑ Reflect on the difference between speaking truth to power and being a tattletale. When have you been truthful and when have you been a tattle?

❑ How is the good news coded in our language today? Look at a worship bulletin from your congregation's worship service. How would an unchurched person visiting your church understand what was going on in worship? Are there any directions? Is everyone expected to know words like *invocation, doxology,* and *benediction*? Are "code words" such as *regeneration* or *sanctification* used regularly? If this is a problem in your worship community, what can be done to change it?

❑ How do you treat your Bible? As an old friend? As a sacred object? Why? Share how you feel about the books of the Apocrypha. Do you feel the same way as you feel about the books of the Bible? Why or why not?

Prayer Time: Review and update the prayer list, and pray together for the people and situations on the list .

Closing Hymn: Sing together or read the verses of the Irish hymn "Be Thou My Vision" (words on p. 97).

3. Faithful, No Matter What

Check-in Time: Check in with the group and share anything important that happened during the past week.

Centering

Holy Imaging: In Matthew 17, Jesus says, "For truly I tell you, if you have faith the size of a mustard seed, you will say to this mountain, 'Move from here to there,' and it will move; and nothing will be impossible for you." [*pause*] For today's holy image, bring to mind a time when you were wronged, a wrong for which you still carry pain or anger. [*pause*] Now envision Jesus joining you on a stairway that leads down to the place where that hurt or anger is stored. [*pause*] Imagine him going with you down that stairway. [*pause*] Now invite Jesus into that closed place and wait for him outside the door. [*pause*] What is happening with that pain? Do you feel the love of Jesus at work alleviating the pain? [*pause*] Are you now able to forgive the one who wronged you? [*pause*] What does Jesus say to you when he emerges from the place where your hurt was stored? [*pause*] Open your eyes, look around, become present in this place, and slowly rejoin the group.

Holy Reflecting: In pairs or in the larger group, reflect on the wrongful situation that brought pain into your life. Did you think the pain of this situation was insurmountable? Are you able to find forgiveness for the one who caused the pain? Are you able to acknowledge your part in creating the painful situation? What should you do about it now?

Other Sharing Activities

❏ As a child, what was your favorite fairy tale or children's story? Why was it your favorite story? Now think of your least favorite story as a child. What caused you to dislike this story?

❏ Think about the places where you grew up. Were there people of other racial, ethnic, or religious backgrounds in your neighborhood? How were they treated by others? by you?

❏ In what ways are Americans called to put allegiance to their country on a par with allegiance to God? Would you be willing to die for your country? Would you die for God's sake? Why or why not?

❏ If you had to name the gods in your life, what would they be? Why would you feel "compelled" to worship these gods?

Prayer Time: Review and update the prayer list. Today use a bidding prayer as your corporate prayer. Have one person offer a short prayer for each person or situation on the prayer list. After each statement, the entire group responds "Hear our prayer, O Lord." For instance, the leader would say "For John who is suffering from cancer, we offer this prayer for healing," and the group would respond "Hear our prayer, O Lord." Be sure to include prayers of thanksgiving and praise as well.

Closing Hymn: Sing together or read the verses to the hymn "Help Us Accept Each Other."

4. Hearing the Truth

Check-in Time: Check in and share with the group anything important that happened to you during the past week.

Centering

Holy Imaging: Paul, in his beautiful description of the "gift of love" in 1 Corinthians 13, says, "Love is patient, love is kind, love is not envious or boastful or arrogant or rude . . . but rejoices in the truth." [*pause*] Now bring to mind a recurring dream you have had that comes out of a dark period in your life. If you have not had such a dream, imagine you are having one now about that dark period. [*pause*] Coming from deep within the subconscious, dreams usually reflect the truth, albeit often in a distorted manner. What "truth" do you think this dream is telling about you? [*pause*] How did you come out of this dark period in your life? [*pause*] How does the healing you have experienced since that time affirm that God's love rejoices in the truth? [*pause*] Open your eyes, look around, become present in this place, and slowly rejoin the group.

Holy Reflecting: In pairs or in the larger group, share as much of your dream as you feel comfortable sharing with others. What truth did you identify about yourself during the holy imaging? How were you freed from the dark time of your life? In what ways does the outcome of your dream confirm that God's love rejoices in the truth?

Other Sharing Activities

❏ Tell from memory or read the fairy tale *The Emperor's New Clothes.* How is this a story of truth-telling? Tell about a time you discovered a lie or helped expose a lie.

❏ Reflect on whether or not it is possible to lie to God.

❏ Has one of your loved ones died before you were able to tell him or her an important truth? Spend time in a prayer of confession, offering the truth now.

Prayer Time: Review and update the prayer list. After praying for each person or situation on your prayer list, conclude your prayer time by meditating on each word of the line in the Lord's Prayer that says "Lead us not into temptation, but deliver us from evil."

Closing Hymn: Sing together or read the verses of the traditional English hymn "The Gift of Love," on p. 98.

5. Your Days Are Numbered

Check-in Time: Check in with the group, sharing anything important that has happened in your life during the past week.

Centering

Holy Imaging: In Exodus 34, God appears before Moses and proclaims, "The Lord, the Lord, a God merciful and gracious, slow to anger, and abounding in steadfast love and faithfulness, keeping steadfast love for the thousandth generation, forgiving iniquity and transgression and sin, yet by no means clearing the guilty, but visiting the iniquity of the parents upon the children and the children's children, to the third and fourth generation." [*pause*] In your mind's eye, recall if there was a time in your life when you were aware you were suffering for the sins of your parents, such as a time when you were treated unfairly, neglected or abused in some way. [*pause*] Remember how you felt at that time. [*pause*] Now picture yourself being held and rocked in the arms of God. [*pause*] What does God say to you? [*pause*] How do you feel now? [*pause*] Allow yourself to feel the comfort and love of God's intimate presence. [*pause*] Open your eyes, look around, become present in this place, and slowly rejoin the group.

Holy Reflecting: In pairs or in the larger group, share the images that came to mind. Then describe the feelings you experienced when the images appeared in your mind. How did it feel to be held and rocked in God's arms and to hear God's words? How can you be God's instrument to help others have this same experience?

Other Sharing Activities

❑ Reflect silently on your sins that will be visited on future generations. Confess these privately to God.

❑ Write blessings for future generations who will live with the consequences of your generation's acts and decisions. Consider writing these blessings on greeting cards for children who are baptized or consecrated in your congregation.

❑ Make up ethical wills. What would you like to leave to future generations in terms of values, politics, economics, faith? Work on the list as a group. Put it in someone's hands to present to the youth in your congregation.

Prayer Time: After reviewing and updating your prayer list, ask one member of the group to read Psalm 57:1-3, one line at a time. After each line, the group will repeat the line, listening for those words that express their own prayers.

Select one line or phrase from Psalm 57 to be the focus of your prayers. Quickly memorize that line or phrase; then close your eyes and repeat it silently, prayerfully to yourself, over and over.

After this time of silent prayer, take turns speaking your line or phrase aloud. It's fine if two people speak the same line. Close the time of prayer with the entire group praying the complete psalm in unison.

Closing Hymn: Sing together or read the verses of the powerful hymn "On Eagle's Wings" or other favorite hymn of God's care and support.

6. The Lion's Den

Check-in Time: Check in with the group, sharing anything important that happened in your life during the past week.

Centering

Holy Imaging: Isaiah 65 contains a beautiful description of God's glorious new creation. As verses 17-25 are being read aloud, picture the description in your mind. Then have someone read the same passage aloud again, pausing long enough at the end of each verse for group members to focus on the images presented in the verse. At the end of the reading, open your eyes, look around, and slowly rejoin the group.

Holy Reflecting: In pairs or in the larger group, share the images that came to your mind. Which image was most meaningful to you? Why was it so full of meaning? Describe how you imagined a wolf and a lamb feeding together and a lion eating straw like the ox. Apart from Isaiah, how do you picture peace?

Other Sharing Activities

❑ Meditate on religious persecution going on in the world today, from church burnings to holy war. Write a litany by making a list of persecutions, and after each one, write "God save us." Pray the litany together.

❑ Talk about what purpose God might have in letting us or others suffer under persecution. Also talk about what responsibilities God gives us to end persecution. Pray for the persecuted.

❑ Draw, sculpt, or photograph your image of the lion and the lamb in Isaiah 65.

Prayer Time: Review and update the prayer list. Then stand in a circle. Read the "Prayers of the Gathered Community" on pages 93-94. Follow the directions in brackets. Then pray silent prayers for those on your prayer list.

Closing Hymn: Sing together or read the verses of the Native American hymn "Many and Great, O God" (p. 99) or another hymn of praise for God's greatness.

7. God of All History—The Ancient of Days

Check-in Time: Check in with the group, sharing anything important that has happened to you during the past week.

Centering

Holy Imaging: There is a wonderfully comforting image of Jesus found in the tenth chapter of John's Gospel. It reads: "Very truly, I tell you, I am the gate for the sheep. All who came before me are thieves and bandits; but the sheep did not listen to them. I am the gate. Whoever enters by me will be saved, and will come in and go out and find pasture. The thief comes only to steal and kill and destroy. I came that they may have life and have it abundantly." [*pause*] Now bring to mind the memory of a time in your life about which you sometimes dream. It may be a difficult time: the death of a loved one or a time of personal challenge or crisis. Or it may be a joyous time: the birth of a child or grandchild or a significant personal achievement. [*pause*] Now picture Jesus joining you in this dream, telling you that he has come to make your life more abundant. [*pause*] Now in your mind let your dream unfold according to Jesus' promise. [*pause*] Open your eyes, look around, and slowly rejoin the group.

Holy Reflecting: In pairs or in the larger group, share the memories of dreams that came to mind. Tell about your recurring dream. What situations or conditions in your day-to-day life cause you to have this dream, such as anxiety, anticipation, exhaustion, or depression? How did the dream change when you imagined Jesus present with you? How does your recognition of the presence of Jesus make your day-to-day life more abundant? How will you react differently to the trials and joys of life?

Other Sharing Activities

❑ Cut pictures from a variety of magazines and make a collage that is dreamlike, perhaps even illustrating a particular dream in an "apocalyptic" fashion. Tell the group about your collage.

❏ Even though they are not real people, tell which characters in books or movies have had a major impact on your thinking. Why?

❏ What has been the most important historical event in your lifetime (e.g., Pearl Harbor, President Kennedy's assassination, the moon walk, a natural disaster)? What were you doing when this event occurred? Why do you suppose you so vividly remember what you were doing when this event occurred? From your perspective, how was God active (or silent) in this event?

Prayer Time: Review and update the prayer list. Choose a name or situation from the prayer list that no one else has chosen. Choose more than one if necessary. Take turns saying sentence prayers for the name or situation you have chosen from the prayer list. Close by dividing into two groups to recite the Responsive Prayer on page 95.

Closing Hymn: Sing together or read the verses of the great old hymn "How Firm a Foundation" (p. 100).

8. The Fall of Babylon

Check-in Time: Check in with the group, sharing anything important that happened to you during the past week.

Centering

Holy Imaging: In Galatians 3, Paul describes new life in Christ: "As many of you as were baptized into Christ have clothed yourselves with Christ. There is no longer Jew or Greek, there is no longer slave or free, there is no longer male and female; for all of you are one in Christ Jesus." [*pause*] In your imagination, look in on yourself standing in the busiest spot you know, such as a street corner, a school, a mall, or a church. [*pause*] Who are the many different people who pass by? [*pause*] Picture yourself as one in Jesus with those around you. Spend a few moments experiencing what it is like to be one in Christ Jesus. [*pause*] Open your eyes, look around, and slowly rejoin the group.

Holy Reflecting: In pairs or in the larger group, share your experience of becoming one in Christ Jesus. How easy or difficult was it to picture yourself from a distance? Who were some of the people who passed by? Were you able to see yourself as one with all of them? What was that experience like for you? How is your vision an apocalyptic vision?

Other Sharing Activities

❏ On a 3" x 5" card, write "It would surprise you to know about me that .
. . ." At the bottom of the card write "My name is . . . ." Write down one
surprising fact about yourself on the card and put your name at the
bottom without showing the card to anyone else. Turn the cards in to a
group leader who, after shuffling them, will read each fact, asking the
group to guess which member's name appears at the bottom.

❏ Reflect on your decision to be a Christian. Did you respond to a
message that said "You'd better believe in Jesus or you'll go to hell,"
or did you respond to the message that says "Have I got good news
for you!" Why? Is the apocalyptic message a threat or a promise?
Why?

❏ In this chapter the author says "there is no limit to the length God
will go to in order to save us and our supposed enemies." Share with
the group who your enemies are. Also think about whose enemy you
might be. Pray silently for forgiveness.

Prayer Time: Review and update the prayer list. Today use a bidding
prayer as your corporate prayer. Have one person offer a short prayer
for each person or situation on the prayer list. After each statement the
entire group will respond "Hear our prayer, O Lord." Be sure to include
prayers of thanksgiving and praise as well.

Closing Hymn: Sing together or read the verses of the Korean hymn
"God Made All People of the World" or the great hymn "In Christ There
Is No East or West."

9. Daniel's Prayer for the People

Check-in Time: Check in with the group, sharing anything important
that happened in your life during the past week.

Centering

Holy Imaging: Jesus taught his disciples a great deal about prayer.
According to Matthew 7, he said, "Ask, and it will be given you; search,
and you will find; knock, and the door will be opened for you. For
everyone who asks receives, and everyone who searches finds, and for
everyone who knocks, the door will be opened. Is there anyone among
you who, if your child asks for bread, will give a stone? Or if the child
asks for a fish, will give a snake? If you then, who are evil, know how

to give good gifts to your children, how much more will your Father in heaven give good things to those who ask him!" [*pause*] Recall a time in your life when you prayed very hard for something that did not materialize or about something that did not turn out as you asked in prayer. [*pause*] Now focus on what actually did come to pass in that situation. [*pause*] Now imagine God speaking directly to you, explaining to you why your prayer was not answered the way you hoped it would be. What does God say to you? [*pause*] How do God's words make you feel now? [*pause*] When you are ready, open your eyes, look around, and slowly rejoin the group.

Holy Reflecting: In pairs or in the larger group, share as much of your unfulfilled prayer request as is comfortable. How was your life affected or changed when the prayer was not answered as you had hoped? Share with one another what you heard God saying to you about the situation and how you felt upon hearing God's words. Now think of times your prayers were answered as you hoped and share those with one another. What does this exercise tell you about the nature of prayer and of God's presence in our lives?

Other Sharing Activities

❑ Reflect on the following questions. Share your responses.

How do you describe prayer?
To whom do you pray?
When did prayer first become important to you?
How has prayer changed for you?
How do you pray? Do you make up your prayers as you pray, or do you use any standard prayers? Do you use different types of prayers at different times?
Have you had some particularly meaningful prayer experiences?
How long do you pray? How often do you pray?
Do you pray silently or out loud? Do you meditate?
When you pray, do you ask for things? Guidance? Blessings? Forgiveness?
What happens to you during prayer? What about afterward?
Does prayer give you a sense of peace?
Does God "talk" to you? Do you feel God's presence?
Do you get answers to your prayers?
When and how do you pray with others? In large or small groups? With a prayer partner?
How does your prayer affect your relationship with other people?

How does your prayer affect your work?

How does your prayer relate to the broader community? society? social justice?

How would you feel if someone asked you to "please teach me how to pray"?

What supports you in your prayer life?

How would you respond if someone asked you, "Are you a prayerful person?"

Prayer Time: Review and update the prayer list. Choose a name from the prayer list for whom to pray and, with eyes closed, take turns saying sentence prayers for each name or situation. Open your eyes and look around at the others in the group. Conclude by having someone guide the group through the Guided Prayer on pages 95-96. Join hands in a circle.

Closing Hymn: Sing together or read the verses to the beautiful hymn "Seek Ye First."

10. Happy Are Those Who Persevere

Check-in Time: Check in with the group, sharing anything important that happened in your life during the past week.

Centering

Holy Imaging: We have come to the end of our study on Daniel. You have each persevered. It has not always been easy, but true to God's promise, we have been rewarded for our perseverance. Listen now to God's promise in Isaiah 40 to those who persevere. "Have you not known? Have you not heard? The Lord is the everlasting God, the Creator of the ends of the earth. He does not faint or grow weary; his understanding is unsearchable. He gives power to the faint and strengthens the powerless. Even youths will faint and be weary, and the young will fall exhausted; but those who wait for the Lord shall renew their strength, they shall mount up with wings like eagles, they shall run and not be weary, they shall walk and not faint." [*pause*] In Holy Imaging in session 1, you were asked to picture yourself moving toward a difficult situation or dilemma you were facing, or were about to face in the near future, or had faced in the past. Bring that image to mind once again. [*pause*] Now picture how that situation has unfolded or how your image of it has changed in the past ten weeks. [*pause*] As you did in the first sessions, picture Jesus joining you to see how that situation unfolded. [*pause*] What does Jesus say to you this time? [*pause*] How do you respond? [*pause*] Allow yourself to walk for some time with Jesus, enjoying the ease and reassurance of his presence with you. [*pause*] When you are ready, open your eyes, look around, and slowly rejoin the group.

Holy Reflecting: In pairs or in the larger group, share how you now see the difficult place or situation you first brought to mind ten weeks ago. How has your situation changed in the past ten weeks? Why do you think it changed this way? What did Jesus have to say to you this time? Is it different from the first time you imaged being together and talking of this situation? How did you respond to Jesus? Why did you respond this way? How did it feel to walk in the presence of Jesus once again?

Other Sharing Activities

❑ Tell about Christians you have known from other countries or who spoke other languages. How were you alike? How were you different? What is your vision for the church in the wider world? How can we, or should we, work together?

❑ Divide into two groups, those who like to be prepared all the time and those who like to prepare at the last minute. Draw up words of advice for the other group and present them.

❑ Write biblical prophecies for each other. For example, "In the fullness of time, you will experience the love of God in new ways" or "Your endurance will pay off in the long run and you will understand God's plan for you." Give your prophecies to each other as a parting gift.

Prayer Time: Review and update the prayer list, making special note of those situations about which you want to continue praying. Have someone write down the following scripture references, each on a separate slip of paper, and drop them in a hat or envelope. In another hat or envelope, put slips of paper, each with a name of someone in the group. Pass the containers, drawing a name and a scripture reference. If you select your own name, draw again. Take turns reading scriptures, inserting the name of the person you drew. When everyone has had a turn, end the prayer time with a prayer of thanksgiving for each person in your group.

John 15:16-17	Isaiah 42:1
Isaiah 43:1-4	Deuteronomy 30:19-20
Jeremiah 29:11-13	Isaiah 41:13
John 15:9, 11-12	Isaiah 44:1-3

Closing Hymn: Sing together or read the verses to the powerful hymn "On Eagle's Wings" or the wonderful anthem entitled "Jesus, Be Jesus in Me."

General Sharing and Prayer Resources

Forming a Covenant Group

Covenant Expectations

Covenant-making is significant throughout the biblical story. God made covenants with Noah, Abraham, and Moses. Jeremiah spoke about God making a covenant with the people, "written on the heart." In the New Testament, Jesus was identified as the mediator of the new covenant, and the early believers lived out of covenant relationships. Throughout history people have lived in covenant relationship with God and within community.

Christians today also covenant with God and make commitments to each other. Such covenants help believers live out their faith. God's empowerment comes to them as they gather in covenant communities to pray and study, share and receive, reflect and act.

People of the Covenant is a program that is anchored in this covenantal history of God's people. It is a network of covenantal relationships. Denominations, districts or regions, congregations, small groups, and individuals all make covenants. Covenant group members commit themselves to the mission statement, seeking to become more...

— biblically informed so they better understand the revelation of God;
— globally aware so they know themselves to be better connected with all of God's world;
— relationally sensitive to God, self, and others.

The Burlap Cross Symbol

The imperfections of the burlap cross, its rough texture and unrefined fabric, the interweaving of threads, the uniqueness of each strand, are elements that are present within the covenant group. The people in the groups are imperfect, unpolished, interrelated with each other, yet still unique beings.

The shape that this collection of imperfect threads creates is the cross, symbolizing for all Christians the resurrection and presence of Christ our Savior. A covenant group is something akin to this burlap cross. It unites common, ordinary people and sends them out again in all directions to be in the world.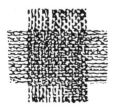

A Litany of Commitment

All: *We are a people of the covenant; out of our commitment to Christ, we seek to become:*

Group 1:   more biblically informed so we understand better God's revelation;

Group 2:   more globally aware so we know ourselves connected with all of God's people;

Group 1:   more relationally sensitive to God, self, and others.

All: *We are a people of the covenant; we promise:*

Group 2:   to seek ways of living out and sharing our faith;

Group 1:   to participate actively in congregational life;

Group 2:   to be open to the leading of the Spirit in our lives.

All: *We are a people of the covenant; we commit ourselves:*

Group 1:   to attend each group meeting, so far as possible;

Group 2:   to prepare through Bible study, prayer, and action;

Group 1:   to share thoughts and feelings, as appropriate;

Group 2:   to encourage each other on our faith journeys.

All: *We are a people of the covenant.*

Music for Meditation

Any good music store will have a section devoted to religious and/or meditative music where these selections may be found.

The Pachelbel Canon with Ocean Sounds by Anastasi Mavrides (Real Music)

Music to Disappear In by Raphael (Hearts of Space)

Music to Disappear In II by Raphael (Hearts of Space)

Ocean Dreams by Dean Evenson (Dean Evenson)

Cristofaros Dream by David Lanz (Narada Productions, Inc.)

Prayers of the Gathered Community

One:

Let us be silent as we face our center.

Let us face East. [*group faces east*]

From the East come desert silences and humble service.

All:

Enable us, O God, to be wise in our actions

and in our use of the resources of the earth,

sharing them in justice, partaking of them in gratitude.

[*group faces the center*]

One:
Let us face South. [*group faces south*]
From the south come guidance and the beginning and end of life.

All:
May we walk good paths, O God,
living on the earth as sisters and brothers should,
rejoicing in one another's blessings, sympathizing in one
    another's sorrows,
together looking to you, seeking the new heaven and earth.

[*group faces the center*]

One:
From the West come purifying waters. [*group faces west*]

All:
We pray that water might be pure and available to all,
and that we, too, may be purified
so that life may be sustained and nurtured
over the entire face of the earth.

[*group faces the center*]

One:
Let us face North. [*group faces north*]
From the North come strong winds and gentle breezes.

All:
May the air we breathe be purified,
and may our lives feel that breath of the Spirit,
strengthening and encouraging us.

[*group faces the center*]

One:
If we walked a path in each direction, the sacred paths
    would form a cross.

All:
And returning to the center, we discover Christ,
who calls us and challenges us.

Original source unknown. Adapted by June A. Gibble.

Responsive Prayer

Leader:
We move so fast, God, and sometimes we see so little in our daily travels. Slow us down. Create in us a desire to pause. Help us to pursue moments of contemplation. Help us to see in a deeper way, to become more aware of the things that speak to us of beauty and truth.

Group 1:
Our inner eye gets misty, clouded over, dulled. We need to see in a new way, to dust off our hearts, to perceive what is truly of value, and to find the deeper meaning in our lives.

Group 2:
All of our ordinary moments are means of entering into a more significant relationship with you, God. In the midst of those very common happenings, you are ready to speak your words of love to us, if only we will recognize your presence.

Group 1:
Teach us how to enjoy being. Encourage us to be present to the gifts that are ours. May we be more fully aware of our senses; sharpen our perception of our everyday treasures and lead us to greater joy and gratitude.

Group 2:
Grant us the courage to be our true selves. Help us to let go of being overly concerned about what others think of us or of how successful we are. May our inner freedom be strengthened and our delight in life be activated.

All:
Life is meant to be celebrated, enjoyed, delighted in, and embraced in all its mystery. Draw us to your playground of creation, God of Life, so that we will live more fully. Amen!

Guided Prayer

Look around you, friends. Look around you.
Who is the person sitting next to you?

The person next to you is the greatest miracle and the greatest mystery you will ever meet. At this moment a testament of the Word made flesh and of God's continuing Advent into the world in our midst.

The person next to you has unlimited possibilities that have only been partially seen.

The person next to you is a unique universe of experience, dread and desire, smiles and frowns, laughter and tears, fears and hopes, all struggling for expression.

The person next to you is striving to become someone, to arrive at some destination, to know and to be known.

The person next to you believes in something valuable, stands for something, works toward something, waits for something.

The person next to you is a whole city of people met during their lifetime. Really a community in which still lives a mother and a father, an enemy and a friend.

The person next to you has something they can do better than anyone else: there is something their one life on earth means and stands for, but dare they speak of these things to you?

The person next to you can live with you and not just along side you. They can live not only for themselves, but also for you. They can confront, encounter, and understand you and be understood in return, if that is what you want.

Be Thou My Vision

Be thou my vision, O Lord of my heart;
naught be all else to me, save that thou art
thou my best though by day or by night,
waking or sleeping, thy presence my light.

Be thou my wisdom, and thou my true word;
I ever with thee and thou with me, Lord;
thou my redeemer, my love thou has won,
thou in me dwelling, and I with thee one.

Riches I heed not, nor vain, empty praise,
thou mine inheritance, now and always;
thou and thou only, first in my heart,
Great God of heaven, my treasure thou art.

Great God of heaven, my victory won,
may I reach heaven's joys, O bright heaven's Sun!
Heart of my own heart, whatever befall,
still be my vision, O Ruler of all.

8th-century Irish song

Daniel

The Gift of Love

Words and Music: Hal Hopson
Copyright © 1972 Hope Publishing Co., Carol Stream, IL 60188. All rights reserved.
Used by permission.

Many and Great, O God

1 Man - y and great, O God, are your works,
2 Great un - to us com - mun - ion with you,

Mak - er of earth and sky Your hands have
O star - a - bid - ing One. Come un - to

set the heav - ens with stars; your fin - gers spread the
us and dwell with us; with you are found the

moun - tains and plains. Lo, at your word the wa - ters were
gifts of life. Bless us with life that has no

formed; deep seas o - bey your voice.
end, e - ter - nal life with you.

Text: Joseph R. Renville, 1846
Music: Plains Indian melody

How Firm a Foundation

1 How firm a foun - da - tion, ye saints of the Lord,
2 "Fear not, I am with thee; O be not dis - mayed,
3 "When through the deep wa - ters I call thee to go,
4 "When through fi - ery tri - als thy path - way shall lie,
5 "The soul that on Je - sus still leans for re - pose,

1 is laid for your faith in his ex - cel - lent Word!
2 for I am thy God, and will still give thee aid.
3 the riv - ers of sor - row shall not o - ver - flow,
4 my grace, all - suf - fi - cient, shall be thy sup - ply.
5 I will not, I will not de - sert to its foes.

1 What more can he say than to you he hath said,
2 I'll strength - en thee, help thee, and cause thee to stand,
3 for I will be with thee, thy trou - bles to bless,
4 The flame shall not hurt thee. I on - ly de - sign
5 That soul, though all hell should en - deav - or to shake,

1 to you who for ref - uge to Je - sus have fled?
2 up - held by my right - eous, om - nip - o - tent hand.
3 and sanc - ti - fy to thee thy deep - est dis - tress.
4 thy dross to con - sume, and thy gold to re - fine.
5 I'll nev - er, no nev - er, no nev - er for - sake!"

Text: "K" in John Rippon's *Selection of Hymns*
Music: American folk melody

Other Covenant Bible Studies

1 Corinthians: The Community Struggles (Inhauser) $5.95
Abundant Living: Wellness from a Biblical Perspective
    (Rosenberger) $4.95
Biblical Imagery for God (Bucher) $5.95
Covenant People (Heckman/Gibble) $5.95
Ephesians: Reconciled in Christ (Ritchey Martin) $5.95
Esther (Roop) $5.95
The Gospel of Mark (Ramirez) $5.95
In the Beginning (Kuroiwa) $5.95
James: Faith in Action (Young) $5.95
Jonah: God's Global Reach (Bowser) $4.95
The Life of David (Fourman) $4.95
The Lord's Prayer (Rosenberger) $4.95
Love and Justice (O'Diam) $4.95
Many Cultures, One in Christ (Garber) $5.95
Mystery and Glory in John's Gospel (Fry) $5.95
Paul's Prison Letters (Bynum) $5.95
Presence and Power (Dell) $4.95
The Prophecy of Amos and Hosea (Bucher) $5.95
Psalms (Bowman) $4.95
Real Families: From Patriarchs to Prime Time (Dubble) $5.95
Revelation: Hope for the World in Troubled Times (Lowery) $5.95
Sermon on the Mount (Bowman) $4.95
A Spirituality of Compassion: Studies in Luke $5.95
    (Finney/Martin) $5.95
When God Calls (Jessup) $5.95
Wisdom (Bowman) $5.95

To place an order, call Brethren Press toll-free Monday through Friday, 8 A.M. to 4 P.M., at **800-441-3712**, or fax an order to **800-667-8188** twenty-four hours a day. Shipping and handling will be added to each order. For a full description of each title, ask for a free catalog of these and other Brethren Press titles.

Visa and MasterCard accepted. Prices subject to change.

Brethren Press® • *faithQuest*® • 1451 Dundee Ave., Elgin, IL 60120-1694
800-441-3712 (orders) • 800-667-8188